JIM McMAHON'S
IN-YOUR-FACE

BOOK OF PRO FOOTBALL TRIVIA

JIM McMAHON'S
IN-YOUR-FACE
BOOK OF PRO FOOTBALL TRIVIA

JIM McMAHON
WITH DAVE BROWN

Contemporary Books

Chicago   New York   San Francisco   Lisbon   London   Madrid   Mexico City
Milan   New Delhi   San Juan   Seoul   Singapore   Sydney   Toronto

The *McGraw·Hill* Companies

Library of Congress Cataloging-in-Publication Data

McMahon, Jim, 1959–
    Jim McMahon's in-your-face book of pro football trivia / Jim McMahon with
Dave Brown.
        p.   cm.
    ISBN 0-07-141319-7
    1. Football—United States—Miscellanea.   2. National Football League—
Miscellanea.   I. Title: In-your-face book of pro football trivia.   II. Brown,
Dave.   III. Title.

    GV950.5.M36   2003
    796.332'64—dc21   2003040906

1 2 3 4 5 6 7 8 9 0   AGM/AGM   2 1 0 9 8 7 6 5 4 3

ISBN 0-07-141319-7

Interior design by Scott Rattray

McGraw-Hill books are available at special quantity discounts to use as premiums and
sales promotions, or for use in corporate training programs. For more information, please
write to the Director of Special Sales, Professional Publishing, McGraw-Hill, Two Penn
Plaza, New York, NY 10121-2298. Or contact your local bookstore.

This book is printed on acid-free paper.

Also by Jim McMahon

McMahon! (with Bob Verdi)

Also by Dave Brown

The Baseball Trivia Quiz Book
(with Mitch "The Wild Thing" Williams)

Contents

Kudos from the Coach

Listen up, pigskin fans: this book belongs in the Football Hall of Fame thanks to that rabble-rouser Jim McMahon. I knew McMahon could team up with a player to change one of the brilliant plays that I had sent in or pull some crazy stunt in the locker room, but I never figured he would collaborate on an All-Pro trivia book.

Let me tell you, it was an exasperating experience coaching Jim for seven years when he was the Chicago Bears' quarterback. My cardiologist had to increase my medication to make sure McMahon's hell-raising wouldn't give me a heart attack. No question, the guy was a terrific quarterback who played his butt off and hated to lose, but he didn't listen to a damn thing I ever said to him. Man, we argued constantly and, of course, Jim didn't forget to include some of our most heated rhubarbs in this book.

From reading it, though, I was surprised to learn that there are so many other people Jim hated more than he did me. He insults coaches, owners, teammates, opposing players, doctors, trainers—he doesn't spare anybody. He even rips a pizza vendor, for God's sake.

Seriously, if you're a football fan, *Jim McMahon's In-Your-Face Book of Pro Football Trivia* is for you. The questions are entertaining and thought provoking; Jim's stories are outrageous and humorous. So grab a beverage, sit back, and enjoy yourself. You'll have fun for hours. But don't believe everything Jim says about me.

—Mike Ditka
Former NFL Head Coach

Pregame Patter

What's up? Jim McMahon here. You know, the quarterback of the 1985 Super Bowl Champion Chicago Bears with the punk haircut who occasionally would stir up controversy. Like the time I wore a headband during a game, on which as a joke I wrote "Rozelle," the name of the NFL commissioner at the time. The league didn't find it very amusing and slapped me with a $5,000 fine. Hey, whatever happened to freedom of expression?

It was quite an experience playing for the Bears and our superintense coach, Mike Ditka. Johnny Unitas, the Hall of Famer for the Colts, was once quoted as saying, "A quarterback hasn't arrived until he can tell his coach to go to hell." If that's true, I arrived in a hurry. Ditka would call some dopey running play on third and long and I'd call an audible at the line, change the play to a pass, and throw a touchdown. He would be incensed: "What does that little jerk think he's doing, changing my plays?!" Just trying to win the game, Mike.

After I'd given seven years in Chicago, the Bears' owners, the McCaskeys, whom I hadn't exactly seen eye-to-eye with since I trashed them in a book that I coauthored with *Chicago Tribune* sports columnist Bob Verdi after the '85 season, ran me out of town. I spent one forgettable year with the Chargers, beating my head against the wall trying to convince Coach Dan Henning that he wasn't going to win very often with his screwed-up game plan. We went 6–10, and I caught the first plane out of San Diego when the season ended and signed with Philadelphia, where I played for three years. Aside from having to put up with the ego of Randall "Mr. Hollywood" Cunningham, I enjoyed playing for the Eagles with all the characters they had, like Reggie White and Andre Waters. And how I loved those Philly cheesesteaks.

Minnesota was my next stop for one year, followed by a season with the Arizona Cardinals, coached by Buddy Ryan. He was my coach in Philadelphia one season and was the Bears' defensive coordinator the year we won the Super Bowl. He used to bicker with Ditka more than I did. That's really saying something.

I then signed with the Cleveland Browns, which turned out to be a three-month nightmare because of Art Modell, the team's tightwad owner, and the clowns he hired as coach and general manager. I was in such a hurry to get out of Cleveland, I signed with the Packers, whose team and coach Forrest Gregg I despised when I played for the Bears. We won the Super Bowl my second year in Green Bay, and I can tell you the championship rings the team gave us were a lot nicer and more expensive than the ones we got after the Bears won, thanks to those cheapskates, the McCaskeys.

I retired following that season. After 15 years, seven teams, and too many injuries and arguments with coaches, I'd had enough. Since then, I've been taking it easy, devoting most of my time to my two passions in life: my family—wife Nancy and four kids—and my golf game. I fly all over the country, competing in these celebrity golf tournaments, in which I hit the links with former athletes like Charles Barkley, John Elway, and Mike Schmidt.

Another guy I've had the pleasure of playing with in these tournaments is Mitch Williams, "The Wild Thing," that zany, smoke-throwing relief pitcher who used to drive up his manager's blood pressure when he'd walk the bases loaded in the ninth inning and then strike out the side for the save. Mitch pitched for the Phillies in the early 1990s, the same time I was playing for the Eagles. Both our teams played at Veterans Stadium, and I would run into him once in a while on my way out to the field to practice my game—golf, that is. I'd take a bucket of balls out there and tee them up.

Mitchy and I, we've had fun playing in these golf tournaments. He's a good golfer, too. He was telling me about the time that he was even after 17 holes. He'd never shot par for a round, and he could smell it—all he needed was one more par to do it. Too bad he triple-bogeyed 18.

The last time "The Wild Thing" and I were walking the course together, he was talking about this baseball trivia book that he coauthored with this sports nut from Philadelphia named Dave Brown. I dropped my club right in the sand trap when he said that. I mean, Mitch is a nice guy, a good pitcher, but what in the world does he know about baseball trivia—except maybe how many chicken wings John Kruk can eat in one sitting. Mitch explained that Dave did the writing, and all he had to do was tell stories about his playing days—some anecdotes, funny quotes he had heard, stuff like that.

Wait a minute, I thought. I haven't worked on a book in 15 years, and I figure it's about time I did. I asked Mitch where I could find this Brown guy. The next thing I knew, Dave was on a plane to Chicago with his cousin Leslie Henry, who is an Eagles fanatic if you ever saw one. They came over to my house, and we had a good old time hanging out together for a few hours, talking first about my chaotic childhood and college days at Brigham Young, and then moving on to my NFL years. Man, I got on a roll, rattling off amusing anecdotes.

Take my rather rotund teammate on the Bears who once spent $23 on a meal—*at McDonald's*. He probably would have dropped $30 if he had dessert.

The year I was with the Chargers, we had this rookie quarterback, a real country bumpkin, who didn't always spot a receiver wide open downfield, but one morning he didn't miss spotting this big booger on Coach Henning's shirt. He told me about it, and I saw Henning that afternoon at practice, when I was wearing a pair of my fashionable Zubaz pants. The booger was still there. "Nice pants, McMahon," he sneered. "Nice booger, Coach."

And there was the time one training camp when I was with the Eagles that tackle Ron Heller and I went up and down the hallways in the dorm spraying guys' rooms with fire extinguishers. The rest of the team finally figured out that we were the culprits and went out and bought 35 fire extinguishers from Kmart to pay us back. Heller and I were slick, though. We found a room across the hall from Coach Rich Kotite and barricaded ourselves in to avoid the onslaught. I'll tell you, that fire extinguisher battle was a lot more fun than studying our playbooks.

I had a few laughs reading through Mitch's book, but I noticed that he didn't really rip any of his teammates, opponents, or managers. There must have been guys Mitch didn't like, but I guess he was reluctant to slam them in print. Not me. You may have gotten the idea already that if I think a guy deserves to be slammed, I'll do it. Quarterbacks especially got on my nerves.

There was this schmuck from Ohio State that the Colts picked ahead of me in the '82 draft. No candy-coating here—the guy stunk. He lasted three years in the NFL as a backup and threw a total of three touchdown passes. His greatest accomplishment in the pros was being named MVP of the championship game—in the *Arena Football League.*

We had this quarterback on the Bears who was on the team for parts of two seasons. Lousy play-caller. Fair arm. Great brownnoser. Ditka loved him, even invited him over for Thanksgiving dinner. Mike never even had me over for a barbecue.

The quarterback that probably irritated me most was a guy you've had to endure listening to as a broadcaster for the past few years. In the 1985 season, his team was forced to use him as a punter once, and he boomed this high, towering kick—it went *one yard*. I could punt the ball farther than that sitting down. Later that season, he had the gall to say—even though he'd never met me—that I wasn't a good role model. After we won the Super Bowl, I went on "The Tonight Show," and Johnny Carson asked me how I felt about this idiot saying I wasn't a good role model. I told Johnny, "I don't listen to anybody who can't punt the ball longer than one yard."

When I was finished telling all my best stories and bashing people I didn't like, I handed the ball off to Dave. Stats and trivia are his bag, so he took all my fine material and wove it into his questions. For example, Dave happened to know that this receiver I threw to on the Vikings had a streak of catching at least one pass in 105 straight games. The only streak of his I remember was during this card game on a plane when he and a couple of other Vikes took me for $700 in *10 minutes*. I made it a point never to play cards with them again.

Dave reminded me that this Eagles running back that I played with set a record by gaining at least 90 yards on a run, pass reception, and kickoff return in the same season. He was also an exercise fanatic who usually did 1,000 sit-ups in *a day*. Wow! I don't think I ever did 1,000 sit-ups in *a decade*.

By the time Dave and I reached the goal line, we had 200 entertaining football questions about everybody from current stars like Marshall Faulk and Peyton Manning and guys I knocked heads with such as Charles Haley and Howie Long to old-timers including Dick Butkus and my favorite player growing up, Joe Namath. Much as I had to keep the defense guessing whether we were going to run the ball or pass, Dave and I keep you on your toes by throwing you a variety of questions; some are of the "who am I?" variety, and the rest are a "mixed bag"—multiple choice, matching, short answer—all the kinds of questions I got wrong when I was in school.

And when I called a passing play, I couldn't keep dumping the ball off to my backs every time—that would be too predictable, and Ditka would have yelled at me for not going long once in a while. I had to keep the defense off balance. So we're opening things up with 50 easy ones, screen passes wide open, and following them up with 50 down-and-outs to the sideline. The second half, we're going to make things tough and fire 50 slants across the middle, and then for the final 50, you will be pushed to the limit when we send you deep into double coverage.

All right, football fans, go to it. I have to practice my putting.

—Jim McMahon

Acknowledgments

Work on this book began at our 10-yard line and the drive downfield for a touchdown required the efforts of many people, whom I would like to thank. Ron Howard, Philadelphia Eagles Director of Marketing/Communications, took the initial handoff by putting me in touch with Jim's longtime lawyer, agent, and friend, Steve Zucker, and his wife, Shelly. I got the project off the ground with their able assistance, and they get credit for picking up a couple of key first downs. My cousin Leslie Henry made a big catch near midfield by teaming up with me for the interview of Mac. Once I started to write the book, my former secretary Maria Costa joined the huddle to type the manuscript, which involved the formidable tasks of understanding my dictation and deciphering my handwriting. She handled the job commendably and advanced the ball several yards. As we neared field-goal range, another former secretary of mine, Teresa Kielburger, was called in for her computer know-how, and she gained some tough yards on the ground. Soon after, we faced a big third-and-long at the 32-yard line and Rob Taylor (at the time an editor for Contemporary Books) made a leaping grab across the middle in double coverage, broke some tackles, and was brought down at the 19-yard line after making the first down. Inside the red zone, we brought in the big guns from Contemporary: editors Matthew Carnicelli, Michele Pezzutti, and Julia Anderson Bauer, as well as editorial assistant Mandy Huber. They dazzled the defense with their editorial expertise and excellent work on the book, and five plays later we were in the end zone for six points. Throughout the drive, my agent, John Sammis, opened up big holes with a lot of blocks.

When you're playing at home, it's a huge help to hear cheering from the crowd, which was enthusiastically provided from the first snap to the goal line by my family, friends, and coworkers. First, big thanks to my lovely new bride, Kimberley (I'll make a sports fan out of her yet), and her great family—parents, Ken and Diane Minch, and brother, Kenny. As always, my gratitude to my family: parents, Bob and Nancy Brown; brother, Doug, and his girl-friend, Patti Spaniak (who is very much part of the family); sister, Kristin Warren, her husband, Fred, and their sons, Greg and Sam. Thanks again to the many friends whom I acknowledged in my earlier baseball book, as well as the following friends who have lent their much-appreciated support: Rebecca Blodgett, Michael and Jane Brophy, Diana Cassel, Chuck and Suzanne Cutshall, Kathy Donohue, Mike Driscoll, Bill and Kathy Glas, Tammy Goff, Ruth Imperato, Barbara Kelvin, Cliff Kilkenny, Claire Kruger, Suzanne Kunkle, Alicia Lyman, Dan and Kirsten McCurdy, Peggy Mercer, Jeff Mitchell, Margie Riehl, Laurie Russen, Cathy Schloth, Kim Walter, Tom Walter, and Dave Weltz. And I certainly can't forget the encouragement I've received from my past and present coworkers, namely, Mike Levin (who has been kind enough to employ me for more than a decade) as well as Eileen Berky, Irina Bernier, Arlene Bogdanoff, Anne Hendricks, Paul Lalley, Edna Long, Kathy McCarthy, Allison Petersen, Rand Prince, Lou Rosen, Andria Saia, Karen Schaeffer, Stacy Smith, and Jaime Weissman.

And finally, while the individuals I have saluted contributed substantially to the touchdown drive, it was Jimmy Mac who engineered the 90-yard march down the field by picking apart the defense with his amusing anecdotes and scathing sarcasm. The team is pleased to award the game ball to him and his gracious wife, Nancy.

—Dave Brown

JIM McMAHON'S
IN-YOUR-FACE
BOOK OF PRO FOOTBALL TRIVIA

Screen Passes Wide Open

Who Am I?

🏈 **1.** Jim paid me quite a compliment when he said that, pound for pound, I was the strongest guy he ever played with. I weighed only 210 pounds, but I could bench press 390, which means I could lie on my back and lift teammate William "the Refrigerator" Perry in the air while he was carrying a 15-pound bag of potato chips in each arm. Lifting weights wasn't really my bag, anyway; running the football was. I rolled up 10 1,000-yard seasons in my 13-year career, scored 110 touchdowns on the ground, and set the record for most yards rushing in a game with 275, which Corey Dillon broke in 2000 when he ran for 278 yards. After I retired, the NFL honored me by inducting me into the Hall of Fame, and the Bears honored me by retiring my No. 34. Who am I?

🏈 **2.** I may never have won a Super Bowl like Terry Bradshaw, Joe Montana, or Troy Aikman, but my name is plastered all over the NFL record books. I rank number one in lifetime touchdown passes with 420 (Fran Tarkenton is a distant second with 342) and am first in career yards with 61,361, almost 10,000 more than runner-up John Elway. Some of my other records include 13 400-yard passing games and 21 four-touchdown performances. Having a lot of great receivers throughout the years such as Mark Duper, Mark Clayton, Irving Fryar, and O. J. McDuffie sure helped. Who am I?

3. On my list of character references, you won't see Jim McMahon's name. He thought I was a self-centered, materialistic, unsociable crybaby. It's not like I always talked about myself or money—when I had my tailor come to the locker room to fit me for my new $1,500 suit, I usually talked clothes. I had my share of detractors besides Jim, especially those fickle Philadelphia fans, whom I played before for several years, hearing a mixture of cheers and boos. I racked up some pretty respectable numbers for the Birds, throwing 20 or more touchdowns four straight years (1987–90) and leading the team—including the running backs—in rushing all four seasons. I was inconsistent, though, and I didn't take it well when Coach Rich Kotite benched me in favor of Rodney Peete early in the 1995 season. Being a backup was such a blow to my ego that I retired after that season, but I reconsidered a year later and had the best season of my career for the Vikings in 1998. Who am I?

4. My coach for the Houston Oilers the first three years of my NFL career, Bum Phillips, had quite an original and amusing sense of humor. When asked why he took his wife with him to road games, Bum joked, "She's too ugly to kiss good-bye." He used to wear his 10-gallon hat during games—except when we played at a domed stadium. How come? "My mother always told me not to wear a hat indoors." When posed the question of whether I was in a class by myself as a running back, Bum praised me in his inimitable way by saying, "I don't know if he's in a class by himself, but whatever class he's in, it doesn't take long to call the roll." The Oilers traded a bunch of draft picks and tight end Jimmie Giles for the number one pick in the 1978 draft, which they used to select me, after I had won the Heisman Trophy for the University of Texas in 1977. I really piled up the yards in Houston; my first five full years (excluding the strike-shortened 1982 season), I averaged 1,550 yards rushing and 13 touchdowns. I carried the ball a whole lot those years—about 345 times a season. Did that concern Bum? "Naah, the ball's not that heavy." My excessive workload, along with injuries, eventually wore me down, and I retired by the time I was 30. Who am I?

5. I worked out religiously, never ate junk food, and had a hard time sleeping—which are three things I did *not* have in common with Jimmy Mac. To maintain my washboard waist, I did 1,000 sit-ups daily—that's 1,000 more per day than Jim felt like doing. I would buy a lot of my food at the health-food store and would see Mac next door at Taco Bell. And while I was an insomniac, Jim never had any difficulty sleeping, especially when there was an early morning practice he wasn't in the mood to attend. I played on the Eagles with Jim one year, 1992, the last of his three years in Philly and the first of my three. I rushed for 1,070 yards and eight touchdowns. In 1993, I ran for 746 yards and also caught 75 passes. And for the Eagles in 1994, I was playing only part-time, but I became the first player in NFL history to have a run from scrimmage, pass reception, and kickoff return of 90 yards or more in the same season. My best year in the NFL was 1988 when I gained 1,514 yards on the ground for the Cowboys, but that was a long way from the 2,411 yards I racked up for the New Jersey Generals of the old USFL in 1985. Who am I?

6. Good thing I liked warm weather all year-round. I was born in southern California, attended high school in southern California, played college ball in southern California (at the University of Southern California, in fact), and spent most of my NFL career with a team in southern California. And quite a career it was, especially early on. After winning the Rookie of the Year in 1982 (I won the Heisman Trophy the year before) by running for 697 yards and a league-leading 11 touchdowns, I rattled off three consecutive 1,000-yard seasons—the last of which I led the NFL with 1,759 yards on the ground and was tied for the AFC lead with 11 touchdowns rushing. I never reached the 1,000-yard plateau again, but I consistently finished with between

700 and 900 yards and maintained my knack for finding the end zone. I finally left California for a team in the Midwest in 1993 and stayed there five years, scoring 47 touchdowns and bringing my career total to 145, which today ranks number three on the all-time list. Who am I?

7. When 20-year-old Mickey Mantle took over the starting center-field job for the Yankees in 1952, he was filling some mighty big shoes—those of "the Yankee Clipper," the legendary Joe DiMaggio, who had retired the previous season. Mick obviously wasn't too fazed by the pressure because he went out and had himself a pretty exceptional career—better than Joe D., some would say. I felt the same kind of pressure that Mickey did in 1991 when Joe Montana, who had led the 49ers to four Super Bowl championships, was battling injuries and close to the end of his career, and I took over as starting quarterback. I guess I responded as well as Mantle did. From 1991 through 1998, I was the NFL's top-rated quarterback six years and led the league in completion percentage and touchdown passes five and four times respectively. In 1994, my completion percentage was 70.3—third best ever for a quarterback in a season—and we won the Super Bowl. Despite that win, my critics claimed that I didn't have the knack for winning the big game like Joe did. The Cowboys eliminated us from the play-offs each of the two years before the Super Bowl season; the Packers beat us in the postseason both of the years after. I hung up my cleats after the 1999 season, and in my retirement speech, one of the guys I thanked was Jim McMahon, who taught me a few things about quarterbacking when we were teammates at BYU for two years in the early 1980s. Who am I?

8. I don't like to toot my own horn, so I'll quote a recent media guide of my longtime team. I have "an incredible combination of speed, strength, and desire" and am "considered by many as the best linebacker in football and one of the best in NFL history." Why all the accolades? In 2000, I was named to the NFL's All-Decade team for the 1990s by the Pro Football Hall of Fame, and in 2002 I became only the second player ever to be voted to the Pro Bowl 12 consecutive seasons. Each season, I usually lead my team in tackles, defense a lot of passes, throw in a few sacks, intercept a pass, force a fumble, recover a fumble or two, and even block a punt or field goal now and then if I'm in the mood. I wish my team could have fared better over the years—we've had only a handful of winning seasons, although we made it to the Super Bowl one of those years. And we have had some bad years, but nothing like the 1–15 season we suffered through in 2000. I was born and spent most of my childhood in the same city in which I have played my NFL ball, but I spent a few years when I was young living in Samoa. My given name is Tiaina, after my father, but nobody calls me that. Who am I?

9. Who holds the record for most yards rushing over a three-year period? Did I hear you say Barry Sanders? Good guess, but not right—he's third with 5,106 (1995–97). Eric

Dickerson? Close, but no go. His 5,147 yards (1983–85) rank second—to me. In three successive seasons, I ran for 1,538, 1,750, and 2,008 yards for a total of 5,296 yards. I was no stranger to the end zone, either—I scored 49 touchdowns on the ground during those years. I also have two Super Bowl rings, and in one of the games I was named MVP after I ran for three touchdowns and 157 yards. Boy, what were those NFL teams thinking about when they passed on me until the *196th* pick in the draft? Who am I?

◄🏈► **10.** Mac watched me on the tube a lot when he was growing up and thought that I was the best linebacker he ever saw. "He knocked the crap out of opposing players, he spit on them, he bit them." Yes, I did—and I sure had fun doing it. They didn't call me the "Maestro of Mayhem" for nothing. The Bears had a field day in the draft following the 1964 season, as they picked Gale Sayers out of Kansas and me out of Illinois in the first round. I was All-Pro seven of my nine NFL years, but unfortunately, like Gale, a knee injury ended my career early. Many years after I retired, I wrote a book about my career that was appropriately entitled *Flesh and Blood*. Who am I?

◄🏈► **11.** My career got off to a blazing start. In 2000, I became the first running back in history to carry the ball at least 300 times in each of his first five seasons and the second back to rush for 1,200 or more yards in each of his first five years. I won Rookie of the Year honors in 1996 and was named AFC Player of the Year in 2000, as I ran for 1,509 yards and 14 touchdowns. I have done some of my best work against the Raiders: I gained a career high 216 yards on the ground against them on opening day of the '97 season and had my second best rushing output against Oakland with 199 yards in a '99 game. Later that season, my team made it to the Super Bowl, which made me the ninth player to win the Heisman Trophy and play in a Super Bowl. I grew up in the Philadelphia area and went to high school my freshman and sophomore years in Abington (which I understand is a stone's throw from the coauthor's office) before I transferred to Fork Union Military Academy in Virginia, where Vinny Testaverde had graduated 10 years earlier. And let's not forget about my acting—I've made television appearances on WB's "In the House" (1997) and CBS's "Nash Bridges" (1998) and hope to do more of that. Who am I?

◀● I 2. I was the leader of those fine Eagles teams in the late 1980s and early 1990s—both on the field and in the locker room. As an ordained minister, I felt it was my duty to help my teammates become better players *and* better people. I had a bunch of the guys on the right track until we were joined by the disruptive presence of Jim McMahon in 1990. Old Jim, he used to hang centerfolds in his locker. "I need them to get me through the day," he'd say. And I would make an announcement after practice, "Bible study meeting tonight at 7:00!" Wise guy McMahon would blurt out, "*Penthouse* Forum study meeting tonight at 7:30!" Jim and I may have had slightly different philosophies on life, but I liked him because he played the game hard and hated to lose, same as me. Those first-round play-off losses when I was on the Eagles really hurt, which made it all the sweeter when the Packers, whom I signed with in 1993, won the Super Bowl following the 1996 season. One of my teammates on the Pack that year was Jimmy Mac. I think it was God's will that brought us back together on the same team again. Jim was always good at avoiding getting sacked, while doing the sacking was my specialty—I'm the NFL's all-time sack leader with 198, and in fact I'm the all-time leader in that category for both the Eagles and Packers. Jim used to say that I threw 325-pound linemen around like they were nobody's business. I enjoyed disposing of offensive linemen and dropping quarterbacks so much, I had the darnedest time quitting. I initially retired after the '97 season, but I decided I'd hang in there another year for Green Bay. After the '98 season, I said that this was definitely it, at 37, and announced my retirement for the second time. What do you know—a year and a half later, I had the fire again to sack the passer, and I played the 2000 season for the Panthers. Retirement speech number three followed the season, and this time, I promise, it's final. Who am I?

13. In 2002, I retired at the age of 42 after an exceptional 20-year career as a cornerback. I hold the NFL record for the most consecutive seasons with an interception—19—as I picked off at least one pass every year except my last one. And, by the way, it was all with the same team. Two of those years, 1992 and 1997, my streak was on the line as I entered the last game of the season without an interception. Both years, though, I came through with one in the finale to keep the streak alive. The interception in '97 was dramatic: I picked off a Bobby Hoying pass and returned it 83 yards for a touchdown, which helped us beat the Eagles, 35–32. I tallied 54 career picks, plus five more in the postseason, including one in Super Bowl XXVI against the Bills. I never snagged one of Jimmy Mac's throws, although I returned a punt for a touchdown against his Bears in the divisional play-offs following the 1987 season. Jim referred to me as "the Shadow" because I was able to stay with the man I defended no matter how good his moves were. My speed helped, too—while I lost a step or two as the years passed, in my prime, I could run the 100-meter dash in 10.08, not far behind Carl Lewis, and in 1991 I was named "World's Fastest Athlete." Who am I?

◀🏈▶ **14.** If I weren't so persistent, my football career might not have gotten off the ground, and I probably would have tried to put my college degree to use and find a job in business. The Cowboys drafted me as a wide receiver in 1992 out of Jackson State, but I broke my leg in training camp; I played only seven regular-season games and didn't catch any passes. The next year I had an emergency appendectomy two weeks before opening day, and I was on injured reserve the whole season. The Cowboys must have thought I was damaged goods because they released me right before training camp in '94, and I signed with the Eagles. I had a decent preseason, but Rich Kotite cut me loose one day after final cuts, and I was out of football the whole year. So my career wasn't off to an auspicious start: three years and zero catches. Things have to get better, I told myself—and they did, better than I could have imagined. I signed with an AFC team in '95 and finally broke the ice by catching 22 passes and three touchdowns and even returning a kickoff all the way. I then stepped my game up a few notches. Over the next six years (1996–2001), I had the most catches and yards of any receiver in the NFL. In '99, I caught 116 passes for 1,636 yards; I almost matched those numbers in '01 with 112 catches and 1,373 yards. They call me "Lightning" and another excellent receiver, who was my teammate for a few years, "Thunder." Who am I?

15. I hold a record that's going to be tougher to beat than some of the eating records of "the Refrigerator"—I played for Super Bowl winners in four different cities. A linebacker out of Penn State, I was drafted in the second round by the Oakland Raiders in 1980, and my rookie year we beat the Eagles in the Super Bowl. After a lengthy legal battle, owner Al Davis moved his team down the coast to Los Angeles after the '81 season, and our second year in L.A., we brought the city a Super Bowl championship. After nine years with the Raiders, I signed with the 49ers in '89, and we went the distance that year. Two years later, I was a Redskin and closed out my NFL career by collecting a fourth Super Bowl ring. I then went to the broadcast booth for nine years, the last six as Dick Stockton's color man, but I got the itch for another Super Bowl ring and in January 2001 was named by a team—that had yet to win a Super Bowl—as their president and CEO. It was tough times for us my first year on the job, as we lost our first 12 and found ourselves the butt of many a Jay Leno joke. And finally, because this is Jimmy Mac's book, I ought to say a few words about him. Hell of a quarterback, that guy—he should have been the starter in Philly over Randall Cunningham. When I was with the Redskins and we played the Eagles, I used to tell my teammates, "Don't knock Randall out of the game because Mac will come in." Who am I?

16. A couple of dozen quarterbacks have won the Super Bowl, but I think I'm the only one who publicly "guaranteed" a victory. That took plenty of balls, incidentally, because my team was a *17*-point underdog. It was January 1969, the week before Super Bowl III. I had led my AFL team to the championship, and I was sick and tired of hearing how much better our NFL opponent was than our team and how they were going to kick our asses all over the field. So I told a room full of people at an awards dinner that we were going to win the Super Bowl—and did we? You're damn right we did—16–7. It was that kind of confidence that Mac admired when he was watching me as a kid, and of course he also liked my flashy wardrobe. On the field I wore my stylish white cleats, and off the field I used to break out my expensive fur coat. Mac thought I could play some ball, too. He said I had the best arm he ever saw and that I could "throw the hell out of the ball." In my heyday from the mid-1960s to the early 1970s, I used to throw 50-yard bullets to receivers like Don Maynard, George Sauer, and Richard Caster. I even threw a touchdown pass to Bobby Brady when I starred on an episode of "The Brady Bunch" in 1973. My career was good on the whole, but it would have been better had it not been for my knee problems, which required multiple surgeries. My knees were so wobbly late in my career, I couldn't run a lick, and if a defender was bearing down on me, I had no choice but to eat the ball. Who am I?

17. Philadelphia drafted me out of Ohio State in the 1987 supplemental draft, and I stepped into their starting lineup my second year, catching 39 passes and 6 touchdowns, and then improved my numbers in 1989 with 45 receptions and 11 touchdowns. I appeared to be an up-and-coming star but surprisingly was waived after the 1989 season. The brilliant rationale of Eagles coach Buddy Ryan was, "All he does is catch touchdowns." I signed with an NFC team, and all I did over the next several years was become one of the greatest receivers of all time: I made 75 or more receptions eight straight seasons, including 122 in back-to-back years; scored at least 10 touchdowns five years in a row with a high of 17; and am second to Jerry Rice in career receptions and receiving touchdowns. It's also worth mentioning that I was selected to the All-Madden team one year as well as Howie Long's Tough Guys of the Millennium, and I am a shoo-in to be elected to the Hall of Fame. Whatever happened to Buddy, anyway? Who am I?

18. Remember the class of '83, that impressive crop of quarterbacks that included John Elway, Dan Marino, Ken O'Brien, Tony Eason, Todd Blackledge, and me? We all went in the first round of the NFL draft that year. The other five guys signed with the NFL team that picked them, but I got offered more money by the Houston Gamblers and tore up the USFL for two years, throwing 83 touchdown passes. Early in 1986, the Gamblers traded me to the New Jersey Generals, but the USFL halted play before I ever played a down for Donald Trump's team. The league filed this big antitrust lawsuit against the NFL in federal court in which they claimed losses of more than $500 million, but because in that type of suit damages could be trebled, the USFL was looking for $1.7 billion. After an 11-week trial, a jury shot down their claims and awarded the USFL one dollar. Luckily for them, they were entitled to treble damages, so that brought the verdict all the way up to three bucks. That definitely was the final nail in the USFL's coffin, and I signed with the NFL team that had drafted me three years earlier. The team was coming off consecutive 2–14 seasons, and attendance jumped 30,000 per game after I signed. I gave them their money's worth. I was their starting quarterback for the next 11 seasons, and year after year, with a swagger that some people didn't like, I got the job done. I led my team to a few divisional titles, completed 60 percent of my passes, and averaged more than 3,000 yards and 20 touchdown passes per season. I did just about it all—except win a Super Bowl. Like Mac, I retired after the '96 season. Five years later, at the age of 40, I wasn't impressed with the quality of NFL quarterbacks, and I cockily commented, "Give me a month, and I'd be better than 60 percent of these guys." Who am I?

19. How good of a head coach was I? Let me put it this way: out of Don Shula, Tom Landry, Chuck Noll, and me, I had the best regular-season winning percentage, .705, that I compiled over 12 years in the 1960s and 1970s, during which I coached two teams. Don't get me wrong—I'm not trying to say that I was a better coach than they were. Those fellows had a knack for winning in the postseason, which I didn't. I coached my teams into the play-offs seven times, but my troops got bumped in the first game six of those years. The other year, we made it to the Super Bowl but lost. The title of a book that I coauthored in the early '70s reflected my coaching philosophy: *The Future Is Now*. I favored wily, seasoned veterans over promising but inexperienced young players. I assembled so many veterans on the second NFL team I coached that we were aptly nicknamed the "Over-the-Hill Gang." The president of that team, Edward Bennett Williams, cracked that when I was a young boy, my father gave me a six-week-old puppy, and I traded it away for two 12-year-old cats. I sure would have if they could run and block. Who am I?

20. In my rookie year for the St. Louis Cardinals, 1972, I did something that nobody in the history of football has done—I gained 98 yards on a play from scrimmage but did *not* score a touchdown. In a game against the Rams, we took the ball on our 1-yard line, and our quarterback Jim Hart hit me with a pass across the middle. I saw some daylight, and it looked like I was going to go the distance, but I was dragged down at the 1. So I went from one 1-yard line to the other. After the season, in which I caught 29 passes for 500 yards, I legally changed my name—both first and last. With my new name, I had another decent year for the Cardinals and one for the Bills, but I really cranked things up when I landed with the Vikings in 1976. With first Fran Tarkenton and then Tommy Kramer throwing the ball and the dangerous Sammy White as the Vikes' other wideout, I averaged 63 catches and 875 yards from 1976 to 1981, which were very strong numbers back then. When I retired, I went into broadcasting, and people have told me that I'm one of the best in the business. As comfortable and polished as I am in front of the camera, my wife has me beat. She's been an actress for many years; you remember her most as Bill Cosby's wife in the long-running hit "Cosby." Who am I? And for extra credit, who *was* I? (What was my name before I changed it?)

◄💬▶ 21. My mom and dad were proud parents on draft day in 1997: two of their sons were picked by NFL teams. In the second round, the Giants picked me out of the University of Virginia, and a round later, the Buccaneers grabbed my twin brother, who was my high school and college teammate. Although our father, James, played briefly in the old World Football League in the 1970s, he didn't make it to the NFL, and he was so thrilled to see two of his sons get drafted, he was screaming his head off. That reminded our mother of me; the story goes that shortly after I was born, I was screaming my head off (like I was different from any other newborn baby), which prompted her to name me Atiim Kiambu, which means "fiery-tempered king." My brother made quite a racket, too, I heard, but he didn't get any nickname. And when I tell you he and I were exact twins, I mean *exact*. Mom had to write our names on the bottoms of our sneakers so the baby-sitter could tell us apart. An appropriate nickname for me as a teenager and adult would be "Mr. Versatile"—both on and off the field. In 1999, I gained 1,739 all-purpose yards (running, receiving, and kick returning) and then took my game to another level the next year with 2,089 yards. In 2001, I dropped down to a still-strong 1,650 all-purpose yards but shot back up to 1,989 yards in 2002, including 1,387 on the ground. Hey, and I'm not just a jock. I won some awards in high school and college for my academics, and since I've been in the NFL, I've worked as a television sportscaster and hosted a radio show in New York. My brother also has versatility— at least on the field. He has scored a touchdown on an interception return, punt return, and fumble recovery, and tied for the league lead of 10 interceptions in 2001. Who am I?

22. November 28, 1995, was a bittersweet day for Jim. He had just parted ways with the Browns after a brief and unpleasant stay and signed with the Packers. "It was so hard to bring myself to being a Packer after I hated them so much when I was with the Bears," remarked Mac. I had also made my way to Green Bay in 1995 via a trade with the Dolphins. We were both back with the Pack in '96 for what would be our final NFL seasons. I was their tight end and didn't waste any time getting down to business, as I caught three touchdown passes in our opening day rout of Tampa Bay. I went on to score 10 touchdowns that year, as we stormed our way to a 13–3 record, then roared through the postseason to win the Super Bowl. Mac and I took our rings and announced our retirements. I was also teammates with Jimmy on the Eagles in 1990 and 1991. I bitched a lot that I wasn't getting paid enough in Philly, which owner Norman Braman got sick of listening to, and I finally left the Eagles and signed with Miami early in the '92 season. I had some productive years in Philadelphia, especially in my rookie year, 1988, when I caught 81 passes. We won the NFC East that year and faced Jim's Bears on New Year's Eve in a first-round play-off game at Solider Field that has been referred to as "the Fog Bowl," because this heavy fog rolled in during the second half that was like nothing the players had ever seen before. I couldn't blame the fog for the first-half pass that I dropped in the end zone—I just couldn't hang on. But that's the kind of day it was, as we squandered opportunity after opportunity. Randall Cunningham threw for more than 400 yards, yet we couldn't crack the goal line once—all we could manage was four field goals, and we lost 20–12. I had some musical ability to go along with my athleticism—I played cello in high school and college. Who am I?

23. Mac, Mike Singletary, Wilber Marshall, and the rest of the Bears were having a rip-roaring time during Super Bowl XX while they were rolling over the Patriots, but I sure wasn't—I was the Pats' head coach who had to endure watching my team get smoked that day, 46–10. Still, I had no complaints—I was thrilled that we made it that far. It was my first full year as an NFL head coach; I replaced Ron Meyer as New England's coach halfway through the '84 season. We made the play-offs as a wild-card in 1985 and had to win three straight games on the road to get to the Super Bowl. I coached four more years in New England before a 5–11 record in '89 did me in. On the whole, I was a good coach but a much better wide receiver, although I wasn't considered a top prospect coming out of college. The Baltimore Colts drafted me in the 20th round in 1954. (With all the NFL teams there are these days, the draft would take a week if they had that many rounds.) I started out as a reserve receiver, but by 1956 I had worked my way into the Colts' starting lineup, as had another player who wasn't a high draft pick. The Steelers picked him in the ninth round of the 1955 draft but cut him even before he took a snap in a preseason game. He didn't hook up with anther NFL team, so in order to stay sharp, he signed with the Bloomfield Rams, a semi-pro team in the Greater Pittsburgh League for the whopping salary of *six dollars* per game. But in 1956, the Colts' GM signed him as a backup quarterback, and he became the starter when the regular was injured. He really showed the Steelers what a mistake they had made, as he held the Colts' quarterbacking job for 17 years, and for the first 12 of those, I was his favorite target. I led the NFL in catches and yards receiving three times each and touchdown receptions twice. I strung together six straight 100-yard games in 1960, which is close to a record. When I retired after the '67 season, I was the all-time leader in receptions with 631, although that record has been broken again and again since. One of the reasons I racked up so many catches was my sure hands—I didn't drop many balls, and I held on to the ones I caught and ran with them. I fumbled only twice in 13 years, which is two fewer times than my Patriots lost the ball in four quarters against the Bears. By the way, that former six-buck-per-game quarterback was the legendary Johnny Unitas. Who am I?

◖█◗ 24. Terry Bradshaw once described me as a quarterback "who went through the fire and survived." The flames of that fire were at their hottest in 1988, my second NFL season for Tampa Bay, when I threw 35 interceptions, second highest season total in history. Especially forgettable games that year were when I was picked four times by the Packers, five by the Eagles, and six by the Vikings. They were all home games, and let me tell you, the boos got loud. But as Terry said, I survived. I gradually cut down on my interceptions in the years that followed, earning respect from those Bucs fans, but then left Tampa Bay in favor of Cleveland. In my second year there, 1994, I led the old Browns to their last postseason appearance and then beat the Patriots before more than 77,000 screaming fans at Municipal Stadium. The team moved to Baltimore in '96, and I put up some career numbers for that city's football-starved fans, who had been without an NFL team for 13 years—I threw for 4,177 yards and tossed 33 touchdowns. I was at my best in 1998 for another AFC team, and maybe that was because I felt so at home; training camp was just minutes away from where I grew up. I hurled 29 touchdowns against just seven interceptions. Those Tampa Bay fans probably couldn't believe it was the same guy. So am I going to the Hall? Probably not, but I've been a warrior: I'm in the all-time top 10 in career passing yards—more than Terry himself as well as some other studs like Phil Simms and Ron Jaworski. Who am I?

25. Mac was teammates with me parts of the 1995 and 1996 seasons, which was not long enough for him to form an opinion as to whether I'm the asshole that so many people think I am. I was originally a first-round pick of the Colts in '89, and I had a solid rookie year, catching 52 passes and four touchdowns. After the season, the Colts packaged me in a big trade to the Falcons, which allowed them to select quarterback Jeff George—another guy who didn't take long to acquire the asshole label—first in the '90 draft. I played five years in Atlanta, and my coaches, teammates, and opponents thought I was an egotistical jerk, which I didn't understand—what's wrong with bragging when you're one of the best? In my five seasons with the Falcons, I averaged 85 catches, 1,125 yards, and 11 touchdowns. I played in the Pro Bowl my first four years in Atlanta but wasn't invited to the game after the '94 season, which was insulting considering the season I put together and that I had been named outstanding player of the previous Pro Bowl. I bounced around from team to team after that, quickly wearing out my welcome wherever I went. One of the stops was in Green Bay as a late-season acquisition in 1996, and I stayed long enough to make my mark: I caught a touchdown against the 49ers in the divisional play-offs and then in the Super Bowl against the Patriots—on the second play from scrimmage, Brett Favre audibled and hit me wide open for a 54-yard touchdown strike. I've done it all, haven't I? They damn well better vote me into the Hall of Fame when I'm eligible. Who am I?

Mixed Bag

◀▩▶ **26.** Michael Jordan carried the Bulls to three straight NBA titles in the early 1990s and then, when he got baseball out of his system, did it again in the late '90s. Close on the heels of the Bulls' second three-year championship run, the Yankees, starring Derek Jeter, Paul O'Neill, and Bernie Williams, won three World Series in a row. But since the Super Bowl kicked off at Memorial Coliseum in Los Angeles in January 1967 (you folks old enough to watch that game will recall that it was known as the AFL-NFL World Championship Game at that time; it wasn't officially called the Super Bowl until the third game), no team has won three straight, although six teams (or seven—one team has done it twice) have come out on top in back-to-back seasons. We respect your football knowledge so much, we have no doubt you'll get six—or all seven—quicker than it used to take Buddy Ryan to chew out a sportswriter for asking what he thought was a stupid question. (You Eagles fans may remember that classic exchange between Buddy and a Philly sportswriter at a press conference after an Eagles loss, which went something like this—Buddy: "Who are you?" Sportswriter: "I'm with the *Philadelphia Inquirer.*" Buddy: "You better inquire somewhere else.") Now, we're going to make you think a little harder. While we're still waiting for the first *team* to win three straight Super Bowls, do you know the first *player* who played—in fact, started and starred—for three straight Super Bowl champions? Here are your choices:

A.   Ken Norton
B.   Dexter Manley
C.   Preston Pearson
D.   Seth Joyner
E.   Earl Morrall

◖▶ **27.** Only the best get the call that they have been inducted into Pro Football's Hall of Fame in Canton, Ohio. For 10 Hall of Famers, we'll give you the player's first and last years in the NFL, primary position(s), and team—either his only team or the team for whom he played most of his career. We don't want to favor younger fans over old-timers, so we're going to go back a few decades. One player retired in the 1940s, one in the 1950s, and two each in the 1960s, 1970s, 1980s, and 1990s.

Player	First Year	Last Year	Position	Team
A.	1932	1941	Fullback	Green Bay Packers
B.	1937	1952	Quarterback	Washington Redskins
C.	1949	1962	Center/linebacker	Philadelphia Eagles
D.	1952	1966	Linebacker	Chicago Bears
E.	1963	1972	Tight end	Baltimore Colts
F.	1967	1977	Cornerback	Detroit Lions
G.	1967	1981	Defensive tackle	Minnesota Vikings
H.	1973	1985	Guard	New England Patriots
I.	1974	1990	Center	Pittsburgh Steelers
J.	1981	1993	Defensive end	Oakland/Los Angeles Raiders

28. Following Jim's senior year at BYU, there were some college All-Star games scheduled mainly to showcase the best players for the upcoming NFL draft. There was a game called the Gold Bowl in warm and sunny San Diego where Jim would have preferred to play, but circumstances were such that instead he flew to Mobile, Alabama, for the Senior Bowl. It was cold and sleeting, and Mac was in no mood to be there. A team meeting was scheduled the morning after he got into town, but due to the consumption of a couple too many adult beverages the night before, he failed to show up. The guy coaching Jim's team, the Kansas City Chiefs' head coach at the time who was scouting for the draft, sent the equipment man up to tell Jim he was late for the meeting, but Jim opted for a little more shut-eye. Jim finally roused himself and made it down for practice, by which time his teammates, in his absence, had voted him captain. The coach apparently didn't care for Jim's lackadaisical attitude and blasted him, "I can't believe you were voted captain! You'll never make it to the NFL!" Jim's curt response: "Don't draft me then." Well, Jim not only made it to the NFL, he was part of a Super Bowl champion team, which his critic at the Senior Bowl wasn't, although he tied a record for most Super Bowls *lost* as a coach. Name him.

◀📕▶ **29.** Not all Super Bowl champions are quarter-backed by a future Hall of Famer like Johnny Unitas or Joe Montana. Several teams have won the big game with a signal caller that was not considered a superstar. Four of the following quarterbacks led their squads to the pinnacle. Which one never won the Vince Lombardi trophy? And for the other four, what team did they lead, and which Super Bowl(s) did they win?

A. Jeff Hostetler
B. Marc Rypien
C. Jim Plunkett
D. Bernie Kosar
E. Doug Williams

◀📕▶ **30.** If you have remained a die-hard fan of this team over the years, you are to be commended for your loyalty. Since their NFL debut in 1966 as an expansion team, they have posted winning seasons about a quarter of the time. Thirteen times, this club has finished the year with four or fewer wins. They have a mere two divisional titles and four postseason victories to their credit. Some of their best players have included William Andrews, John Zook, and Tommy Nobis. Can you name this team?

31. Even though the Bears accumulated 46 points in Super Bowl XX against the Patriots—which was a record at the time—the MVP was awarded not to one of the offensive players but to one of the team's defensive stars. After all, the Bears' D held the Patriots to 123 yards (just 7 rushing) and created six turnovers. Through the 2003 game, that was one of only seven times in Super Bowl history in which a defensive player has won the MVP. We'll give you the year of the Super Bowl, his team, his position, and something about his performance that day. You give us the players.

Player	Year (No.)	Team	Position	Performance
A.	1971 (V)	Dallas Cowboys	Linebacker	Only player to win MVP for losing team
B.	1973 (VII)	Miami Dolphins	Safety	Intercepted twice, once in the end zone to thwart drive
C.	1978 (XII)	Dallas Cowboys	Defensive end/ defensive tackle (co-MVPs)	Strong rush, contributed to four interceptions and four fumble recoveries
D.	1986 (XX)	Chicago Bears	Defensive end	Credited with 1½ sacks, helped stifle running game
E.	1996 (XXX)	Dallas Cowboys	Cornerback	Made two key second-half interceptions, returning them 44 and 33 yards
F.	2001 (XXXV)	Baltimore Ravens	Linebacker	Spearheaded defense, which held opposing offense scoreless
G.	2003 (XXXVII)	Tampa Bay Buccaneers	Safety	Triggered Bucs' first-half explosion with a pair of kicks

◀🏈▶ **32.** Hey, you might not have liked Jimmy Mac's brashness or his amazing assortment of headbands, but you have to admit, the guy knew how to win football games. During one stretch in the mid-'80s, the Bears won 25 straight games when Ditka started him at quarterback. Over his NFL career, Mac's regular-season record as starting QB was 67–30 for a sizzling .691 percentage. How do other quarterbacks stack up against Jim in that category? Match these active or recently retired signal callers with their regular-season percentages as starting quarterback.

A. .665   Vinny Testaverde

B. .570   Warren Moon

C. .502   Troy Aikman

D. .442   Jeff George

E. .371   Brett Favre

◀🏈▶ **33.** It's one of the most exciting plays in football: a return man receives a kick or punt deep in his own territory, runs it the 25, breaks a couple tackles, finds some daylight, and sprints *all the way* down the sideline for a touchdown. Here are questions about four guys who have been among the best in recent years at electrifying crowds with touchdowns on kick returns.

A. This speedster returned two punts in a game for a touchdown *twice*, in 1993 for the Browns and in 1997 for the Chargers. He also caught 104 passes for the Falcons in 1995.

B. What a year this Heisman Trophy winner from the University of Michigan had with the Packers in 1996. He ran three punts back for touchdowns during the regular season and then was named MVP of the Super Bowl after he set a bundle of return records, including taking a kickoff back 99 yards for a six-pointer.

C. This graduate of Southwestern Louisiana is the king of kick returns—he holds the NFL record for most yards gained on punt returns *and* most yards gained on kickoff returns.

D. This group is on the small side—all are shorter than 6′, and only one weighs more than 190 pounds—but this guy, at 5′9″, 170 pounds when he played, was the smallest. Like the rest, he could really motor, especially on kickoffs as he returned six for TDs; half of those came in 1994 for the Lions. He also took three punts back for scores and led the league in punt return average twice.

◀●▶ 34. Let's get something straight here—Mac's talents are not limited to quarterbacking, golfing, wearing fashionable clothes, and ripping new assholes of guys he doesn't like—he can also act. What a cast he teamed up with in the 1988 movie *Johnny Be Good*: Robert Downey Sr., Robert Downey Jr., Anthony Michael Hall, and Uma Thurman. Mac played—who else?—himself. Numerous other football players have made appearances on the big screen. Try to match these players with the movies—some were football flicks, some weren't—in which they had a role.

A.	*Semi-Tough*	Jim Brown
B.	*The Chamber*	Ray Nitschke
C.	*The Last Boy Scout*	Paul Hornung
D.	*The Dirty Dozen*	Lynn Swann
E.	*The Longest Yard*	Bo Jackson

35. The Bears lead all NFL teams in the retired uniform numbers department with 13 players. Most of the players are old-timers like Bronko Nagurski (No. 3), Bulldog Turner (No. 66), and Red Grange (No. 77). They haven't retired Mac's No. 9 yet, and as long as the McCaskeys own the Bears, you can be sure they won't. Here are 10 quarterbacks whose numbers were retired by their teams. The numbers range from 7 to 22; there are no duplicates. Think hard and see if you can come up with at least eight of the numbers and the teams.

Bart Starr	Joe Montana
Joe Namath	John Elway
Fran Tarkenton	Phil Simms
Bobby Layne	Johnny Unitas
Dan Marino	Dan Fouts

36. Talk about much ado over nothing. This flamboyant, hard-hitting linebacker was the ticket (he sure thought so) when he was laying hits on quarterbacks and running backs for the University of Oklahoma in the mid-'80s. He won the Butkus Award as the nation's outstanding linebacker two years running. The Seahawks picked him in the first round of the 1987 supplemental draft, expecting him to play as well as the man after whom the award was named. They were slightly disappointed. Seahawks teammates M. L. Johnson and David Hollis lasted longer in the NFL than he did. (We're having a hard time remembering them, too.) In defense of the Oklahoma star, it wasn't poor performance that did him in, but a shoulder injury—it limited his pro career to two dozen games and ended it before his 25th birthday. With his football career in the toilet, he took to the screen and starred in some respectable thrillers, including *Stone Cold* and *Blackout*. This is definitely a screen pass wide open, but just in case you're suffering from temporary brain freeze, we'll give you five choices.

A. Craig "Ironhead" Heyward
B. Brian "the Boz" Bosworth
C. Jack "Hacksaw" Reynolds
D. Thomas "Hollywood" Henderson
E. Jack "the Assassin" Tatum

37. Mac's friend and occasional golfing partner Mitch Williams was tagged with the notable nickname of "The Wild Thing" early in his career. When asked whether he liked his nickname, Mitch deadpanned, "People have called me a lot worse things than that." We bet they have.

Football players have acquired some memorable monikers, too. We're going to give you five of these nicknames; for each, we'll give you the duration of the player's career and the team for whom he played all or the majority of his career. Name the player.

Player	Nickname	First Year	Last Year	Team
A.	"the Galloping Ghost"	1925	1934	Chicago Bears
B.	"the Swamp Fox"	1954	1961	Philadelphia Eagles
C.	"the Sundance Kid"	1968	1977	Miami Dolphins
D.	"the Snake"	1970	1984	Oakland Raiders
E.	"the Wizard of Oz"	1978	1990	Cleveland Browns

◀📢▶ **38.** No doubt you and your fellow football junkies have debated over a few cold ones at a pregame tailgate this question: what is the greatest football dynasty of all time? Some of you have argued that the Packers during the 1960s, when Vince Lombardi led them to five championships in eight years, was the premier team ever. The 49ers unquestionably have gotten some votes with the team they put together in the 1980s at Joe Montana's peak when they won four Super Bowls. And if you've done some tailgating in Philadelphia, you've seen a lot of those soft-spoken, well-behaved Eagles fans wearing T-shirts that proclaim: "Dallas Sucks!" But they didn't during a four-year stretch in the 1990s when the Cowboys and their insufferable owner Jerry Jones won it all three out of four years. Hey, but how 'bout those Steelers teams from the 1970s that won the whole ball of wax four out of six years? What a team loaded with stars that coach Chuck Noll had—six of their starters on the Super Bowl winners were later enshrined in the Pro Football Hall of Fame. Two were offensive players; four played D. Each of the six spent his entire career with the Steelers, except one who played 12 years with the Steelers and then spent part of a season with the Seahawks. Name the six stupendous Steelers and the only one who wore something other than black and gold in his career.

39. In case you're getting tired of our long-winded "Who am I" questions and multiple-part doozies that never seem to end, we're going to break things up and toss you one short, garden-variety trivia question: who are the only four head coaches in NFL history to take two different teams to the Super Bowl?

40. Behind every successful man is a good woman—or so they say—and likewise, behind every successful quarterback is a running back who can run the hell out of the ball. Mac will be quick to point out that having his greatness, Walter Payton, in the backfield made him a better QB because if the other team played a pass-prevent defense, Wally would burn them for a long gain. Just as Mac in his Bears days had the luxury of a great running back to terrorize the defense, other quarterbacks were also lucky enough to have a star runner keeping them company. Match these five quarterback–running back tandems.

A.	Wilbert Montgomery	Ron Jaworski
B.	James Brooks	Joe Montana
C.	Kurt Warner	Phil Simms
D.	Roger Craig	Dave Krieg
E.	Joe Morris	Boomer Esiason

41. Mac played three years in Philadelphia. Coauthor Brown, his brother, Doug, and his sister, Kristin, were raised by their parents in the Philly suburbs, as was cousin Leslie; Brown and Doug still live in the area, Kristin has been bugging her husband to move back there for years, the folks always enjoy visiting from South Carolina, and Leslie just moved back after an agonizing 20 years away from the "City of Brotherly Love." We think you know what this question is about—NFL players who were born in Philadelphia.

A. At 6′6″, 325 pounds, this bruiser can match "the Refrigerator" bite-for-bite on a good day. The Jets, the Dolphins, and the expansion Browns employed him to play offensive tackle. He has the same first and last names as a famous musician, a famous football player turned actor, and a well-known football sportscaster.

B. This fellow weighs about half as much as the guy in the previous question, but boy has he made the folks back home proud. From 1999 to 2002, he averaged 117 catches, 1,581 yards, and 13 touchdowns per season. Jerry Rice numbers, wouldn't you say?

C. He went to the same high school in Philadelphia, Simon Gratz, that produced basketball star Rasheed Wallace. A defensive end, he was drafted by the Raiders in 1999 out of East Carolina and played in the AFC Championship Game his second year.

D. This Philly boy played his college ball an hour down Route 95 at the University of Delaware for coach Tubby Raymond, who won his 300th game for the Blue Hens in 2001. His NFL career looked like it was in the tank before he was 30, but he resurrected it and has had strong years at quarterback in his thirties.

E. Finally a suburbanite for you—he went to Pennsbury High in Fairless Hills, Pennsylvania, a northern Philadelphia suburb. He's quite a cornerback, and he set an NFL record in 1996 for the longest interception return for a touchdown, 104 yards (with a lateral from James Willis) for the hometown Eagles.

◀▬▶ 42. We're not sure about this one—you may nail it with a snap of the fingers or you may fire off three or four guesses over a frosty beverage and a hoagie and come up empty-handed. Here goes: what man was a head coach in the NFL for fewer than 15 years and led his team to three Super Bowl victories? No multiple choice here, but in case the right answer is eluding you, we'll toss you some hints. He won the Super Bowl his second year as head man, his second-to-last season, and once in the middle of his 12-year run. He may have been able to win one or two more, but the rigors of being an NFL head coach wore on him, and he stepped down at the age of 52 to pursue other sports-related interests.

◀🏈▶ **43.** One thousand yards in a season for a running back is good, but 1,500 yards is *really* good. In football history, more than 150 guys have reached four figures on the ground, but only about 30 have gone the extra 500 yards. Mac was teammates, at one time or another, with *five* of the 30. Walter "Sweetness" Payton was one, of course; the other four, Mac was teammates with for only a year, and each running back had his 1,500-yard effort another season. In fact, three of the four did it for another team. Two of the four had the big year before they were teammates with Jim, two after. No assholes in the group—Jim would tell you if there were. Let's use a baseball analogy for the scoring: take a base for each 1,500-yard runner you name, so if you hit all four, you have yourself a home run. If you also come up with the years that these runners joined the 1,500-yard club, you have, to take a page out of Chris Berman's book, a "grand salami."

◀🏈▶ **44.** They are the most prolific field-goal kickers in NFL history, as they rank one-two on the all-time list in three-pointers. One is right-footed and slight of build; the other is a stocky lefty. One was born in Denmark, the other in South Africa. Each broke into the NFL in 1982 and was still playing in 2002. Both have been deadly inside the 40-

yard line, but the lefty has been better from long range. In 1998, their teams played each other in the NFC Championship Game. The righty missed a key 38-yard field goal in the fourth quarter that would have clinched the game for his team, and the lefty ended up winning it in overtime with a 38-yarder. You probably know who these guys are by now, but if not, here is a big hint: their last names are pronounced the same, although they are spelled slightly differently.

45. Take a poll of Ohio State Buckeyes football fans and ask them who the best receiver the school ever produced was, and Cris Carter would undoubtedly be the hands-down winner. He had 27 touchdown catches in college (first among Buckeyes receivers) and a whole boatload more in the NFL. (Mac had the privilege of throwing to Carter in '93, his year with the Vikings.) But Carter isn't the only star receiver ever to suit up for the Buckeyes. In the mid-1990s, Ohio State had three receivers that Jim never had the opportunity to send out on a passing play—each had a better rookie year in the NFL than Carter. In 1996, a Buckeye was drafted in the first round by an AFC team, and he set an NFL rookie record by catching 90 passes. When he was a sophomore at OSU in '94, he didn't even *start* because the Buckeyes had two of the top college receivers in the nation. Both were drafted in '95 by AFC teams, one in the first round, the other in the third. The first-round pick became the 10th rookie to roll up 1,000 receiving yards. The third-round pick also broke in with a bang—he caught nine touchdowns and averaged an awesome 23.5 yards per reception.

Name this trio of outstanding Ohio State receivers and the teams who drafted them.

◀▥▶ 46. Even if you hate the Cowboys, their owner Jerry Jones, and all that "America's Team" bullshit, which a lot of people in the country do, including Mac and most of Brown's family, you have to admit they've been a good team most of the time. One of the reasons is that they always seem to be armed with excellent quarterbacks—both starters and backups. We've described five spanning from the early Cowboys days of the 1960s into the turn of the millennium. The more right answers you get, the more you must hate the Cowboys; if you're not remembering these guys, you must be indifferent toward them. Five out of five makes you a full-fledged Cowboys hater.

A. The Cowboys chose this St. Paul, Minnesota, native in the 1989 supplemental draft after they made Troy Aikman the first overall pick in the main draft. That year, he nearly split playing time with Aikman when they were both rookies, but early in the '90 season, he was dealt to the Saints (Ditka hadn't arrived yet) when the Cowboys settled on Troy as their quarterback. He later played for the Bears (by which time Ditka was gone) and the Rams.

B. Who did the bulk of the quarterbacking for Dallas in the 1980s and set the Cowboys' record for touchdown passes in a season in

1983 with 29? A hint: he also handled the team's punting job for a few years while he was there.

C. Aikman was steady and has three Super Bowl rings, but this Navy graduate was probably the Cowboys' best quarterback to date—he was the NFL's top-ranked passer three times in the 1970s. Once, when he was kidded about being straitlaced, especially compared to playboy Joe Namath, the Dallas quarterback quipped, "I enjoy sex just as much as Joe—except it's only with one woman."

D. Who replaced Eddie LeBaron as the Cowboys' starting quarterback in 1963 and held the job for six years? We'll add that he later entertained "Monday Night Football" viewers with his anecdotes and folksy humor while trying to make sure Howard Cosell stayed sober.

E. In the 1990s, Aikman was almost always the man taking the snaps from the Dallas center— he threw almost 4,100 passes. What Cowboy ranked a distant second to Troy in passes in the '90s with 320?

47. These fancy new stadiums that have cost taxpayers hundreds of millions of dollars are impressive, but no doubt many of you old-timers grumble that they don't have the character of the stadiums from a generation or two ago. We've listed five stadiums that NFL teams called home way back before some of you youngsters were born. Match each to the team that played there. If these stadiums are Greek to you, give your father or grandfather a holler, and he should be able to bail you out.

A.	Oakland Raiders	Franklin Field
B.	Philadelphia Eagles	War Memorial Stadium
C.	Buffalo Bills	Frank Youell Field
D.	Pittsburgh Steelers	The Polo Grounds
E.	New York Giants	Forbes Field

48. Who knows why, but trades are much more common in baseball than in football. When players switch teams in football, it's usually via free agency. While baseball has its share of free-agent signings, the owners still like to wheel and deal. Mac was traded once in his NFL career; here are questions about that trade and three other noteworthy football deals.

A. By the time the Bears' training camp opened in 1989, Mac was so exasperated with the shenanigans of the McCaskeys that he wanted out of Chicago—immediately. He got his wish toward the end of camp when he was traded to the Chargers for a second-round pick in the '90 draft. With that pick, the Bears chose a linebacker from Fresno State, who played his first six years in Chicago, mostly as a reserve. Ironically, after the Bears released him, he signed with the Packers, and he and Mac were teammates on the 1996 Super Bowl Championship team. He then went back to the Bears for another year. That's a tough one, unless you're a Bears or Packers fan. Any guesses?

B. Two months after Mac was traded, in October 1989, the Cowboys and Vikings made a trade way too complicated to provide all the details about. It involved 6 players and 12 draft choices, many of which were conditional. The deal became more complicated when one of the players, Darrin Nelson, refused to report to the Cowboys, and he was traded five days later to San Diego, where he became one of Mac's teammates. The key player in the mammoth Minnesota deal was acquired by the Vikings, but he didn't quite do for them what they expected. Name him.

C. What running back did the 49ers pick up in 1978 in exchange for San Francisco's second- and third-round picks in the '78 draft and first-, second-, and fourth-round picks in '79?

D. The Colts dealt this superstar running back for two picks in the April 1999 draft, then picked Edgerrin James a month later in the first round (fourth pick overall) of the draft.

◀🏈▶ **49.** You want to hear an unbelievable stat? Since the landmark merger of the leagues in 1970, nine players have led the NFC or AFC in catches two or more consecutive seasons, yet *none* of the nine is in the top 20 on the all-time list of leaders in receptions. In other words, Jerry Rice never led his conference in catches back-to-back years. Neither did Art Monk, Henry Ellard, James Lofton, or Michael Irvin. Don't get us wrong—it's an impressive group, these nine. We'll give you the team, years, and number of catches; you know what to do from there.

Player	Team	Years	Catches
A.	Oakland Raiders	1971–72	61, 58
B.	Baltimore Colts	1974–75	72, 60
C.	San Diego Chargers	1980–82	89, 88, 54
D.	San Francisco 49ers	1981–82	85, 60
E.	New York Jets	1987–88	68, 93
F.	Houston Oilers	1990–92	74, 100, 90
G.	Green Bay Packers	1992–93	108, 112
H.	Cincinnati Bengals	1995–96	99, 100
I.	Carolina Panthers	1999–2000	96, 102

◀🏈▶ **50.** Brown has had fun writing these sports trivia books with "Mitchy-pooh" (as Phillies' broadcaster Harry Kalas used to call him once in a while) and Jimmy Mac, but he's had to keep his day job as a lawyer all along. We thought a lawyer joke followed by a question about lawyers was in order. All right, what's the difference between a good lawyer and a great lawyer? A good lawyer knows the law; a great lawyer knows the judge. Sad, but true. Here are a few questions about NFL players who have gone to law school or had connections with lawyers.

A. Minnesota may get the award for the state with the most ex-athletes in high-ranking positions. An NFL Hall of Famer (and 1971 Associated Press MVP for the Vikings) tortured himself with three years of law school after his football career and later ascended to the Minnesota Supreme Court. And, of course, there's the former professional wrestler who ended up in the governor's mansion. Who are we talking about besides Jesse Ventura?

B. Which place-kicker from the 1970s and 1980s earned his law degree by taking classes during his off-seasons?

C. For the Eagles in 1991, Randall went down for the season in the opener, and when Mac missed some games with injuries, Coach Rich Kotite practically had to advertise in the Help Wanteds to find a quarterback. Brad Goebel and Pat Ryan were awful (between them they threw 10 interceptions in 82 passes), but another QB played respectably while Mac was healing. He also quarterbacked the Rams, 49ers, and Seahawks earlier in his career. His father called the Bills' signals for a few years in the 1960s, then went to law school, and the next thing you know, he was debating Al Gore. No, it's not W. and his father. Who are they?

D. This cornerback hasn't gone to law school, but in June 2001 he married a lawyer—at least a TV lawyer: former "Law & Order" star Angie Harmon. Name him.

Down-and-Outs to the Sideline

Who Am I?

51. I didn't set any football records, but I must have set an eating record when I spent $23 on a meal—*at McDonald's*. Man, I was so full after that, I almost didn't have room for dessert. When the Bears drafted me as a defensive tackle out of Clemson in 1985, I was a svelte 308 pounds, but inhaling all those Quarter Pounders and loads of other junk food caused me to balloon to 360 by 1987. The Bears tried to get me to shed a few pounds during training camp and served me small pieces of fish and chicken at dinner. They thought I was sticking to their diet until one night at bed check, one of the coaches found pizza boxes and beer bottles stacked up in my dorm room. In the memorable 1985 season, not only did I start at defensive tackle, Mike Ditka came up with this ingenious idea in the middle of the season to use me as a running back down near the goal line. The coach figured, this guy is so huge, he ought to be able to barrel into the end zone from the 1-yard line. Sure enough, I scored two touchdowns on the ground and even caught a TD pass when Jim faked a run to "Sweetness" Payton and found me wide open. The icing on the cake was when I scored a running touchdown against the Patriots in the Super Bowl. Who am I?

52. To come up with my name, you will have to be either a football historian or old enough to collect Social Security. I was an NFL star back in the '30s and '40s in the days of Sammy Baugh and Bronko Nagurski. I was the Jerry Rice of my time—in my 11 years with the Packers, coached by Hall of Famer Curly Lambeau, I led the NFL in touchdown receptions nine seasons, receptions eight times, and yards receiving seven years. Today, all these years later, my 99 touchdown catches still put me fourth on the all-time list. I was such a receiving threat that opposing teams employed something previously unheard of—double- and triple-teaming—but I still piled up the catches and TDs. Curly led our Packers to three championships while I was there, and my average share for winning the title was $950. That's a far cry from the more than $60,000 that each member of the Super Bowl champion pockets these days. By the way, my contribution to the Packers' success wasn't limited only to offense—back in my era, two-way players were the norm, and when the other team had the ball, I played safety—and quite well, especially toward the end of my career. In my last six seasons, I intercepted 30 passes, leading the league one of those years. I even helped out with the Packers' kicking duties a couple years. Hey, even Deion didn't do that. Who am I?

53. The record book reflects that the Bears chose me in the first round of the 1987 draft, but there should be an asterisk that says "picked by Chicago because Jim McMahon refused to piss in a jar." Here is the story: the 1986 season was a nightmare for Jim, as he hurt his shoulder twice; the second injury, in Week 12, knocked him out for the year. Jim was annoyed with the Bears' president, Mike McCaskey, and the team trainer because they didn't take his injuries seriously. In fact, Jim doesn't recall that the trainer gave him so much as an aspirin for his pain. Then, in the off-season, they started making these accusations (which Jim insisted were ridiculous) about him being "dirty with drugs," partly because he sometimes wore dark glasses, although he had worn them since he was six. They made him submit to urine tests to see if he was on drugs and claimed a test was dirty—although they wouldn't show him the results. Jim then had an independent test that proved he was clean. Finally Jim got fed up and told the Bears, "I'm not pissing anymore; find me another team." The Bears said they were drafting a quarterback unless he continued to get tested. Jim wouldn't give in, so the Bears chose me in the first round of the '87 draft. The Bears eventually did trade Jim right before the '89 season to the Chargers, and my playing time increased. By 1990, I was the full-fledged starter and led the team to the play-offs that season and the following year. I later signed with the Colts, and for them in 1995, I was the league's number one passer, as I completed 64 percent of my passes, threw 17 touchdowns, and was intercepted only five times. Who am I?

54. I committed two major faux pas in 1985, my final year in the NFL, and as a result I was slammed on late-night television after the season. I was a quarterback by trade but was called on to punt once by my team, the Redskins, and didn't exactly bury the other team deep in its own territory: I shanked it for a 1-yard punt. We would have been better off trying to get the first down. That same year, the Bears were going undefeated, and their young quarterback, Jim McMahon, was a little too outspoken and flashy for my liking. I said publicly that I didn't think McMahon was a good role model. Never mind that I hadn't even met him and that I wasn't exactly a model husband and father. After the Bears won the Super Bowl, Jim went on the talk show circuit, and "Tonight Show" host Johnny Carson asked him how he felt about my comment. Jim responded, "I don't listen to anybody who can't punt the ball longer than one yard." When I wasn't trying to punt and kept my mouth shut, I did all right for myself. After backing up Sonny Jurgensen and Billy Kilmer in my early years, I took over the Redskins' starting quarterback job in 1978 and held it until my career-ending knee injury, which I sustained on a hit by Lawrence Taylor. I helped the 'Skins beat the Dolphins in Super Bowl XVII, a game in which John Riggins rushed for

166 yards and declared afterward, "Reagan may be president, but today I am king." Who am I?

55. I was teammates with Jimmy Mac in Philadelphia—both on the football field and at the bowling alley. One year during the season, to give us a break from football, about 30 of us Eagles bowled in a league on Monday nights. Jim, Reggie White, and I were on the same team. Mac led the way by averaging 170, I was in the 140s, and Reggie, well, his average wasn't very good, but he definitely was fun to watch—he looked like Fred Flintstone, sliding halfway up the alley as he threw the ball. I didn't take bowling too seriously, but I was all business playing cornerback. I was an All-Pro selection five of my seven years with the Eagles, and one of the seasons, 1993, I tied an NFL record by returning four interceptions for touchdowns. I almost duplicated the feat in 2000 when I had three runbacks for the Raiders. Who am I?

56. I was yet another intense, hard-hitting member of those Eagles defensive units in the Buddy Ryan/Rich Kotite era. I played on the defensive line with Reggie White and the late Jerome Brown. My teammates voted me defensive MVP in 1989 on the strength of my 15½ sacks, and I went on to have All-Pro seasons in 1991 and 1992 when Mac was in town—I had a league-leading 19 sacks in '92. I reunited with Buddy and Jim on the Cardinals in 1994 and finished up with the Bears in 2000. It was a good career—

I really enjoyed sacking all those quarterbacks—and my only regret is that I never played in a Super Bowl. The closest I came was the 1996 AFC Championship Game, but my Jaguars were knocked off, 20–6. A final note of interest: I attended high school in Wilmington, North Carolina, where I played basketball against Michael Jordan and also was a Babe Ruth League teammate of the NBA icon. Who am I?

57. When Mac left Philadelphia after the 1992 season in favor of the Vikings, I filled his spot by signing with the Birds after seven years with the Steelers. The starter, Jim's friend Randall Cunningham, broke his leg in the fourth game of the '93 season, knocking him out for the year. I stepped in and handled the bulk of the Eagles' quarterbacking the rest of the year, and I played pretty well, completing 59 percent of my passes and throwing 14 touchdowns against only five picks. I later played for Denver, where I was John Elway's backup during his last two NFL seasons in which he led us to Super Bowl victories. I had one of my best games as a Bronco in 1998; with Elway sidelined due to an injury, I assumed the job as starter and threw four touchdown passes against my old team, the Eagles. Like Mac, I spent a good deal of time on the baseball diamond growing up; as a matter of fact, after graduating from high school in Monroe, Louisiana, I played a year of minor league ball in the Detroit Tigers' organization. A .180 batting average and no home runs as an outfielder/shortstop convinced me baseball wasn't my game, and I played football at Tulane, then Northeast Louisiana. My mother named me Walter, but you know me by a nickname, which my five older sisters hung on me when I was young. Who am I?

🏈 **58.** I rank up there with Dick Butkus, Ray Nitschke, Lawrence Taylor, and Mike Singletary as one of the greatest linebackers of all time. My nickname, "the Mad Stork," was appropriate, as I covered the field with speed and tenacity and was renowned for my devastating tackles. I spent my early years with the Colts, where I teamed up with defensive stars like Bubba Smith, Jerry Logan, and Mike Curtis. The majority of my career, though, I wore the Raiders' black and silver, and I fit in well with the likes of Lester Hayes, Phil Villapiano, and Jack Tatum. I had some aches and pains, but they didn't keep me off the field on Sunday—I suited up for 215 straight regular-season games, one of the league's longest streaks ever. And when the calendar read January, my season usually wasn't over. I played on four Super Bowl winners (one with the Colts, three with the Raiders) and made eight Pro Bowl appearances. On top of all that, I had a zany sense of humor, which Mac would have appreciated. One year with the Raiders, I made quite the grand entrance our first training camp practice. I rode up, not in a taxi, not in a limo, but on a *horse*, wearing a German helmet and spikes, no less. Who am I?

🏈 **59.** When I got on a hot streak, there wasn't any stopping me or my teammates. In 1986, my Vikings were trailing Philadelphia, 23–0, with eight minutes left in the fourth quarter. Those Eagles thought they had the game wrapped up, but then we put it to 'em and scored four touchdowns—I had two of them—in the last four minutes, and we pulled out a miraculous win, 28–23. That game was early in my streak of 105 straight games of catching at least one pass, which ended in 1992. And then at the beginning of the following season, 1993, a couple of other Vikings receivers, Cris Carter and Jake Reed, and I invited Jimmy Mac, who had signed with the Vikes that year, to a friendly card game called Boo-Ray on a plane ride. Jim might have known how to read a defense, but he couldn't figure out the secret of Boo-Ray. In just 10 minutes, Cris, Jake, and I lightened his wallet by $700. Jim called it quits after that. What else do you want to know about me? I was fourth in the 1981 Heisman Trophy voting, set the NFL record in 1987 for most yards receiving in a postseason game with 227 (which was broken by Eric Moulds in 1998), and closed out my career with the Lions in 1995. Who am I?

◀📰▶ 60. I was the first pick in the entire 1974 NFL draft, which is rather impressive considering that I didn't play high school football. Like Mac, when I was growing up, football wasn't my favorite sport—I spent my time playing hoops in my hometown of Jackson, Tennessee, and was offered 52 college basketball scholarships. I ended up going to Tennessee State, where the football coach convinced me that at 6'9", 270 pounds, I could be quite a force on the defensive line. We lost only one game my three years at Tennessee State, and my Cowboys didn't lose much when I got to the pros. Three of my first five years, we made it to the Super Bowl, winning once. And then, to the surprise of everybody, I pulled a Michael Jordan; I announced I was retiring from football to pursue a career in another sport—not basketball, though—*boxing*. I fought six bouts and won them all, but the competition wasn't exactly Muhammad Ali and Joe Frazier. I decided that I had more fun trying to sack the quarterback than knock some guy out, so I went back to football, where I played another 10 years for the Cowboys. Who am I?

61. There are many men who played for Vikings head coach Dennis Green who regarded him as a top-notch coach and good guy. Jim McMahon is not one of them. Prior to the '93 season, the Vikes signed Mac to a two-year contract. Mac played well, completing 60 percent of his passes, winning 8 of the 12 games he started, and helping Minnesota to the play-offs. After the season, though, Mac was hit with the surprising news that he had been released. So much for the two-year deal. A month later, the Vikings signed quarterback Warren Moon, and one of the first things Green said was, "I have to get Warren an offensive line." Jim's reaction toward Green went something like this: you give me a two-year commitment, the first year the offensive line is one of the team's weaknesses, but I do my best. I win two-thirds of the games I start, we make the play-offs, and after the season you get rid of me and then say, hey, I have to improve our offensive line so our new quarterback will have enough protection—that's bullshit! I can understand how Mac felt. I was on his offensive line that year, and while I pulled my weight, some of the other boys didn't. Mac went so far as to say I'm one of the strongest guys ever to play the game and that I can really manhandle defensive linemen. I could deadlift 620 pounds in college, so containing 300-pound tackles has never been that hard. Here's the irony: my year with Mac, I was named All-Pro for the fifth straight year, and I stretched the streak to 11 through 1999. After the '99 season, I was—can you believe it?—*released* and signed with Tampa Bay. I didn't stick around to hear Green's comments. Who am I?

◀▣▶ **62.** I never made the All-Pro team, but if they voted for an all-time Free-Spirited team, I'd be one of the starting defensive tackles. You can be sure Mac would get the nod as quarterback. I don't rival Mac in the clothes, sunglasses, or one-liner departments, but he didn't have a tarantula and boa constrictor as pets in college, like I did at the University of Pittsburgh with my roommate Burt Grossman. By the way, Burt later played with Mac on the Chargers and earlier went to high school in the next town over from the hometown of Mac's coauthor, Brown. The tarantula and boa certainly made good conversation pieces when we had girls over to the room. I could play some football, too, although my road to the NFL was not all that smooth. First off, wrestling was my bag in high school—at David Brearly Regional High School in Kenilworth, New Jersey, I had a 97–1 record and was New Jersey state champion senior year. When I came out of Pitt, I was passed up in the 1990 draft, but the Colts signed me as a free agent, and I played seven years in Indy. It was then off to Baltimore, where my Ravens were in the middle of the pack my first three years, and then—boom!—out of nowhere, in 2000 we won 12 games during the regular season and rolled over four opponents to win the Super Bowl. I think my arrival at our team's training facility via helicopter for spring minicamp inspired our great season. Incidentally, my wife, Kathy, doesn't let me have a boa constrictor and tarantula anymore (I don't see why not; I think our kids would enjoy playing with them), so I have to settle for a dog (Sambuca) and cat (Parmesan). Who am I?

63. I really hated to lose. Good thing for me, my teams didn't lose much. My first 11 years in the NFL, my numbers went like this. Years my team won at least 10 games: 11. Years my team finished first in the division: 10. My team's regular-season winning percentage: .746. Years my team won the Super Bowl: 5. I spoiled my track record when, after a two-year hiatus, I came back for one more season in 1999, and we went 4–12. Still, I'm the all-time Super Bowl sack leader, and I played in five Pro Bowls as a defensive end. I also had a knack for getting into arguments with my coaches, which is why my first team traded me after the 1991 season. After I retired, I went into coaching, and

I really got a taste of losing my first two years; the Lions, in 2001 and 2002, went 2–14 and 3–13, respectively. Who am I?

◀▥▶ **64.** I knew I had a promising career as a professional athlete when I was named Co–Orange County, California, High School Athlete of the Year in 1993 with Tiger Woods. I starred in football and basketball at Huntington Beach High and the University of California; at Cal, we made the "Sweet 16" my senior year. As much as I enjoy hoops, I was better at football, and with my speed and size (6′4″, 250 pounds) I was a natural for tight end and was grabbed in the first round of the '97 draft. With each year of experience in the NFL, I got better. I made 33 catches my rookie year, improved to 59 the next year, 76 in '99, and in 2000, I caught 93 passes—a franchise record. In 2001, I hauled in 73 more passes. I also set an NFL record in 2000 for most 100-yard receiving games in a season for a tight end with six, which broke the previous record of five held by a bunch of great tight ends, including Kellen Winslow, Pete Retzlaff, and none other than Mike Ditka. I've loved life on the gridiron, but I still have the passion for basketball; often, after I score a touchdown, I dunk the ball over the goal post, and I get to run with some of the current NBA studs in a summer league. Who am I?

◀▥▶ **65.** The groundwork was laid for the Bears' dominating teams of the mid- to late 1980s with a series of strong drafts, starting in 1979. That year Chicago made me, a defensive tackle from the University of Arkansas, the fourth overall pick in the draft (they had acquired the choice in a trade from Tampa Bay), and five picks later snagged Al Harris, a defensive end (who also played some linebacker in the pros) out of Arizona State. I was one of the pillars of the Bears' defense, playing in four Pro Bowls in the 1980s. A fierce competitor and punishing tackler, I earned the nickname "Danimal." Mac will also tell you that I liked to run my mouth and sometimes could get on his nerves. In the 1986 season, he hurt his shoulder in our opening game, and he was missing some games and practices in the weeks that followed. I thought that maybe Mac was making a bigger deal out of his shoulder than he should have, and I rode him about it once in a while. Mac finally had had enough, and after a game, he was in the training room with this huge wraparound zipper on his shoulder, and when I walked in, he snapped, "Hey, this is what they do for you when there's nothing wrong with your shoulder." Mac and I got along well on the whole, though, and I was bummed when he left for the Chargers in '89. I played two more years for the Bears, and that was it for me. Who am I?

66. What do the Jets, Colts, Bucs, Bengals, Redskins, Saints, and Chargers have in common? They all took a look at me and cut me loose in 1978 and 1979, my first two years out of college. Because I was dreading the thought of trying to do something useful with my degree in government from Dartmouth, I decided to make one more go of it, in 1980, and the third time was the charm. I latched on with an AFC team, and I had so much trouble making it past final cuts with the other teams, I figured that I ought to stay a while, so I did—14 years. I became one of the premier NFL kickers, averaging 105 points per season and hitting about 80 percent of my field-goal attempts. The longer, the better was my motto. I connected on two 58-yarders, one from 57, and 19 more from 50 yards plus. I kicked the last three years of my career for the Jets, and for them I averaged only 80 points, which had nothing to do with my efficiency as a kicker but everything to do with the Jets' offense being so crappy—they didn't get into field-goal range much to give me a chance to score three. We won all of 10 games those three years, and those nasty New York fans booed Mac's old Eagles coach Rich Kotite out of town after 3–13 and 1–15 seasons. Bill Parcells came in, and I, along with about half the team, was sent packing. So I was released by the Jets in 1997, 19 years after they had become the first team to release me. My interest in football and government growing up was fueled by conversations I used to have as a kid with my family's next-door neighbor in Washington, D.C.—Byron "Whizzer" White, who as you may know, was an NFL star in the late 1930s and later became a United States Supreme Court Justice. Who am I?

67. I could write an entire question about the sports accomplishments of my family members. I was the ninth of ten children growing up in Everett, Washington. One of my brothers played minor league baseball in the San Francisco Giants' organization. One of my brothers-in-law is Larry Stefankski, the former coach of tennis great John McEnroe and more recently the coach of Yevgeny Kafelnikov. My wife, Diane, was a big-shot tennis player herself at USC, and her father, John Brodie, was the longtime quarterback for the 49ers and played on the Seniors Golf Tour after he retired from football. I play 18 with my father-in-law when I can, and although he gets around the course quicker than most, I usually score more birdies and pars. I'm a scratch golfer and in fact have played in tournaments with Jimmy Mac. I won a long-drive contest once, as I crushed a ball 331 yards. Although I play good golf and also lettered in baseball, basketball, and track in high school, chucking the pigskin has really been my bag. The Colts picked me in the third round of the '88 draft, and I won the starting job my rookie year. Unfortunately, I didn't light the world on fire, spent most of my second year on the bench, and was traded to Tampa Bay after the season. I quickly turned into a journeyman, as I played for my fifth team before I was 30. They traded me to team number six, and it was for them in the late '90s that I put it all together. I had back-to-back Pro Bowl seasons, and in the second of those years, I took my team to the Super Bowl. Finally, I'll tell you that my wife and I have three daughters, and with all the athletes in the family, I'm expecting one of them to grow up to be a great gymnast or skier. Who am I?

68. There was a boatload of Randall Cunningham's qualities that Mac didn't like, and high atop the list was that he whined and pouted like a baby when he didn't get his way. Thankfully, Mac was gone for some time when Randall's whining and pouting were at their worst. Four games into the 1995 season, with the Eagles struggling at 1–3, first-year coach Ray Rhodes benched Randall and handed the quarterbacking job to me. I held the job the rest of the season, and while my stats were nothing special (eight touchdowns, 14 interceptions), I was just the spark that the team needed; as Randall watched from the bench seething, we won 9 of our final 12 to land one of the wild-card spots. We kept the hot streak going in the first-round play-off game against the Lions, exploding for 58 points and advancing to the next round to meet the Cowboys. At about that time, Randall's wife was expecting their first baby, and he stirred up some controversy by threatening to miss the game and fly to Las Vegas to be with his wife if she gave birth. He stayed in town, avoiding a hefty fine from Rhodes, but the Cowboys beat us 30–11. Apparently, Randall was so humiliated by warming the bench most of the season, he retired in the off-season only to be lured out of retirement a year later by Dennis Green. I originally was drafted by Detroit in '89, and I also have seen action for Dallas, Washington, Oakland, and Carolina. My father never played in the NFL, but he was the running backs coach with the Bears for three years in the '90s under Dave Wannstedt. And my wife, Holly Robinson, never had time for sports—she was too busy acting. She starred with Billy Dee Williams (who played Gale Sayers in the classic *Brian's Song*) in *The Jacksons: An American Dream*, a well-reviewed made-for-TV movie that chronicled the lives of Michael Jackson and his siblings. Who am I?

69. I'm in the NFL record books for a couple boneheaded plays. In the fourth quarter of Super Bowl XXVII in January 1993, my Cowboys were putting a hurtin' to the Bills, and I picked up a fumble at our 35-yard line and started lugging my 290-pound body the other way. I had smooth sailing toward the end zone, but at about the 10-yard line, I could smell the end zone and I got careless by slowing down and starting my touchdown celebration by holding the ball up. Don Beebe of the Bills stripped the ball from me right before I was going to score. Good thing we were winning so big; otherwise, Jimmy Johnson would have taken my head off for being so sloppy. By the way, my 64-yard run was the longest fumble return in a Super Bowl. Ten months later, on Thanksgiving Day in '93, we were playing Miami on a snowy, blustery day, and Jimmy did take my head off after that one. We were winning, 14–13, but with less than a minute left in the game, the Dolphins drove and set up for a 41-yard field goal by Pete Stoyanovich. The kick was blocked and started to roll crazily toward our end zone. Nobody had told me the rule that if a field goal is blocked and the ball is touched by a player on the defensive team, it becomes a live ball and the kicking team can retain possession. I tried to fall on the ball but couldn't hang on, and it kept trickling toward our goal line where a Miami player fell on it at the 4-yard line. Stoyanovich then hit a chip shot to win the game for the Dolphins. Take my word for it, Coach Johnson used some four-letter words with me in the locker room, and they weren't, "Nice game, dude." After those two plays, I felt like I needed to redeem myself—and I did. In the next Super Bowl in January 1994, the Bills were beating us by seven points at halftime. In the first minute of the third quarter, I jarred the ball loose from Thurman Thomas, and our safety, James Washington, scooped it up and ran 46 yards for a game-tying touchdown. We went on to win the game, 30–13. All told, I played 10 years for the Cowboys (although my active status was interrupted three times when the league suspended me for overindulging in recreational activities) and made it to the Pro Bowl twice. After my decade in Dallas, I signed as a free agent with an AFC team in 2001. Who am I?

70. In his book *Run to Daylight*, Packers legendary coach Vince Lombardi, for whom I played offensive line in the 1960s, said he regarded me as the finest player he ever coached. I later coached the Packers myself—for four years in the 1980s—and Jim McMahon, whose Bears teams banged heads with us twice a year, thought I was one of the biggest jerks he ever encountered. The feeling was mutual. Whenever we played each other, McMahon and Ditka were always swearing and making obscene gestures toward me. One time, McMahon threw a touchdown pass against us, and he came running off the field, pointing his finger at me, and screaming, "Take that, you sonovabitch!" McMahon and Ditka must have been doing something right because my Packers beat the Bears only once in the eight games we played them. I coached the Packers to an 8–8 record my first two years, and then I really took it on the chin with 4–12 and 5–9–1 seasons. Who am I?

71. There must not have been many NFL scouts who attended my games at Trinity Valley Community College and Texas A&I because all 28 teams passed me up in the 1990 NFL draft. But the Vikings gave me my shot when they signed me as a free agent—and they're damn glad they did. I was a full-time starter by '92, and I strung together eight consecutive 10-sack seasons, second longest streak to Reggie White's nine. My honors with the Vikings included All-Pro (seven times), Pro Bowl invitation (six), NFC Defensive Player of the Month (four), and All-Madden Team (two). Thank you, John. Minnesota released me in March 2001, after 11 seasons and 114 sacks. Three of the quarterbacks high atop my "sacked most" list have Super Bowl rings: Brett Favre, Trent Dilfer, and Steve Young. Two days after the Vikes let me go, I signed with the Seahawks. In my spare time, I like to learn about players around the league by perusing other teams' media guides (while listening to Frank Sinatra), and I read that the guy whose spot I took in Seattle, Cortez Kennedy (they released him five days after signing me), had a career similar to mine. He played for the 'Hawks during the same years that I played for the Vikings (1990–2000), and he played in eight Pro Bowls. Cortez didn't pile up my sack totals, but I must admit, he played the run better than I have. I've told you a lot, and I hope you know my name, and I also hope you remember my older brother Ervin, who was a linebacker for the Bucs and Chiefs from the mid-1980s until the early 1990s. Who am I?

72. Even if you know absolutely nothing about football, you have a shot at this question if you watch soap operas, movies, and music videos and read magazines. I made a cameo, along with a teammate, in the 1996 hit movie *Jerry Maguire* starring Tom Cruise and Cuba Gooding Jr.; appeared in several episodes of "The Young and the Restless" during the 1996 off-season; was featured in a 1998 music video with Toni Braxton; and was listed as one of the country's most eligible bachelors in a 2000 issue of *People* magazine. (Jim's coauthor, Brown, is still fuming he didn't make that list.) Now onto my football career. I didn't play much in my rookie campaign of 1994, but since then my name has been penned regularly into my team's starting lineup, and I've racked up some strong stats. I'm usually good for between 60 and 80 catches, 1,000-plus yards, and a handful of touchdowns each season. My teammate at the time who did the *Jerry Maguire* cameo with me had some even better receiving numbers. And now let's turn to some interesting odds and ends about my family. My mother is Japanese-American, and I attended a Japanese elementary school for three years. My brother broke in as a rookie running back/kick returner for the Saints in 2000 and was traded to the Jets during the 2001 preseason. Another brother earned a degree from Dartmouth in biomedical engineering (he still hasn't explained to us what in God's name that is) and then went on to medical school. Who am I?

73. My mother has always been an avid football fan, which is a good thing for her because she has always been surrounded by football players. Her husband—my father—played in the NFL, as did her two sons, my brother and me. How long did I play in the NFL? Long enough to match my brother's 19 years in the league. Long enough to play in *40* NFL stadiums. Long enough to block for three Heisman Trophy winners, including Mike Rozier. (I also blocked for two in college, including Charles White.) Long enough that one of my teammates in college played in the NFL, retired, went into coaching, and became my head coach. I'm sorry to say, not long enough to play on a Super Bowl champion, although I did play in the big game late in my career. How good was I? I played in 10 Pro Bowls and was invited three other years but was replaced due to injury. And one of my former coaches, Jerry Glanville, hailed me as the "greatest offensive lineman ever." I don't know about that, but it was a nice compliment. Who am I?

74. My road to winning the Heisman Trophy and playing in the NFL was long and winding. In 1989, I was the top-ranked high school quarterback in the nation for Cretin-Derham High in St. Paul, Minnesota, and was bombarded with football scholarships from big-time schools. I initially enrolled at Florida State, but I put football on the back burner and decided—to the shock and against the advice of many—to chase my number one dream of playing major league baseball. The Toronto Blue Jays drafted me, and because I was doggedly determined to make it to the bigs, I spent six years and hundreds of bus rides in their minor league system as a first baseman. While I showed some progress as I advanced to Triple A, I never got the call to the majors, and when I finally realized that I would probably never step foot on a major league diamond, I went back to Florida State to give football another go in '97. It proved to be the right move as I got better each year: in '99, my junior year, I threw 25 TDs and led the Seminoles to the national championship. In 2000, I upped my touchdowns to 33 and passed for more than 4,000 yards, including games of 536, 521, 496, and 443, which earned me the Heisman Trophy plus a bunch of other awards—at the age of 28! Heisman winners are usually gobbled up early in the draft, but because of my age, I wasn't picked until the fourth round. I won the starting job my rookie year in the NFL in 2001, and while my team was lousy and I was inconsistent, I threw for almost 3,000 yards. Who am I?

75. I had one hell of a year in 1997. My team had just won its division with a 13–3 record during the 1996 regular season. In the NFC Championship Game against Carolina, I ran for 88 yards on only 10 carries and caught five passes for 117 yards, including a 29-yard leaping grab for a touchdown and a 66-yard reception that set up a touchdown. In our Super Bowl victory two weeks later, I gained 61 yards on the ground. That fall, in the '97 regular season, I kept on trucking by running for 1,435 yards, and in one half against the Cowboys, I busted out for 145 yards. On an off day, I made an appearance on "Oprah." The topic of discussion: the difficulty of pro athletes finding suitable spouses. That was the year of my life, but the *game* of my life was back in 1988 when I was a senior at Nottingham High School in Syracuse—I scored *seven* touchdowns and kicked eight extra points for a total of 50 points. I think I was named Player of the Game. And for you dog lovers, here's something of interest: I'm co-owner of a company based in Atlanta that offers dog training, breeding, and boarding. Who am I?

Mixed Bag

76. One thousand yards rushing in a season is not quite the accomplishment it used to be. Nowadays 15 to 20 backs each season usually crack the magic number compared to fewer than 5 in the 1960s and about 10 in the 1970s. We think you'll remember most or all of these retired runners who eclipsed the 1,000-yard mark at least once. We're going to give you one of the years that each back gained at least 1,000, his team, final yards total that season, and the number of 1,000-yard seasons he had in his career. You give us their names.

Player	Year	Team	Yards	Career 1,000-Yard Seasons
A.	1964	Cleveland Browns	1,446	7
B.	1975	New York Jets	1,005	5
C.	1983	Los Angeles Rams	1,808	7
D.	1985	Atlanta Falcons	1,719	3
E.	1992	Pittsburgh Steelers	1,690	1
F.	1995	New York Giants	1,182	5

77. How many of those running backs did you remember? If you hit at least four out of six, Jimmy Mac is impressed—he got only three right. If you're one of those fans who pays too much attention to the passing game to notice what the runners are doing and were able to come up with only one or two, here is your chance to redeem yourself. We've listed the same information about six receivers who made it to the 1,000-yard club one or more times. See if you can beat your score on the running backs question.

Player	Year	Team	Yards	Career 1,000-Yard Seasons
A.	1965	Dallas Cowboys	1,003	2
B.	1976	San Diego Chargers	1,056	4
C.	1981	Denver Broncos	1,244	3
D.	1986	Indianapolis Colts	1,131	1

| E. | 1991 | Washington Redskins | 1,340 | 5 |
| F. | 1995 | Detroit Lions | 1,488 | 2 |

78. Jim fit in well with those Bears teams coached by Mike Ditka, but he would have been even a better fit with John Madden's rough and tough Raiders teams of the 1970s. Those boys used to have their share of brushes with the law, and big John sometimes had to come to the rescue and bail them out of jail. In the 1980s, after John had stopped coaching and started broadcasting, he would host a golf tournament one weekend every spring, and many of the old Raiders would attend. Jim was lucky enough to become a regular on the invite list, and he had a great time hanging out with Madden's men. They didn't always play that much golf, but they told funny stories and ran up some monstrous bar bills. Here is info about four guys who played for the Raiders in the 1970s and partied with Jimmy Mac in the 1980s. Who are they?

A. A powerful, hard-nosed fullback, he led the Raiders in yards rushed four straight years (1971–74), topping 1,000 in 1972. Halfbacks that joined him in the backfield included Charlie Smith and Clarence Davis.

B. Jim had a lot of laughs imbibing and trading stories with this giant: he stood 6′8″, weighed 275 pounds, and played defensive end with ferocity. He started as a rookie for Vince Lombardi's Packers in 1961, went to

Washington for two years, and then spent the next eight years with the Raiders.

C. "You should've been a Raider," this 10-year Raiders safety used to tell Jim at the Madden tourneys. He played in the same secondary with Jack Tatum, Willie Brown, and Dave Grayson. In his career, he intercepted 30 passes and scored seven touchdowns.

D. His bald head and fondness for cognac were two trademarks of this seven-year Raiders defensive lineman. He was one of a very small handful of NFL players who didn't play college football, although his offbeat personality prompted "Monday Night Football" broadcaster Alex Karras to joke that he attended the University of Mars.

79. Mike Ditka had a string of five straight winning years for the Bears in the 1980s. It was a good run by Mike, but a long way from the record. Can you pick out the man from these five legends who coached his team to an amazing *20* consecutive winning seasons?

A. Paul Brown
B. Chuck Noll
C. George Halas
D. Tom Landry
E. Don Shula

80. Despite some star-studded teams over the years, this club's frustrated fans have watched all too many 6–10, 7–9, 8–8, and 9–7 seasons. Only twice through 2002 have they won 10 or more games in a season. John Yarno and Blair Bush have played center for them. Their all-time roster of defensive linemen includes Manu Tuiasosopo and Natu Tuatagaloa. John Leypoldt and Ruben Rodriguez have at times handled special team duties. And if those clues haven't helped you out much, this one probably won't either: Gale Gilbert played backup quarterback for a while. Name the team.

81. You've been watching the Super Bowl every year as long as you can remember, right? So you ought to know what team pulled the game out with a last-minute touchdown, who took a lead into the locker room at halftime only to get smoked in the second half, and which team's offense always goes to sleep in the Super Bowl. Let's see if you do. Which team in the Super Bowl . . .

A. scored 31 points and lost?
B. scored 14 points and won?
C. has tallied a paltry 34 points in four Super Bowl appearances?
D. put the game-winning touchdown on the board with 34 seconds remaining in the fourth quarter?
E. led the game at halftime but lost by 19 points?

82. You probably had to put down your beverage and really think on a couple of those, especially the last one. These are easier, no doubt. We'll be disappointed if you don't rattle off at least four correct answers. We're looking for quarterbacks who accomplished rather impressive feats in the Super Bowl. A hint to start you off—the answer to one is Jimmy Mac. Which quarterback in the Super Bowl . . .

    A. threw six touchdowns in one game?
    B. was named MVP in the last game of his career?
    C. ran for two touchdowns in one game?
    D. was voted the game's MVP three times?
    E. threw four touchdown passes in one *quarter*?

83. We've been peppering you with so many questions about the Super Bowl, you'd think we forgot that there were NFL Championship Games before the Packers and Chiefs knocked heads in the first Super Bowl following the 1966 season. The prior 33 seasons, dating back to 1933, the winners of the Eastern and Western Divisions/Conferences played each other to decide the NFL Championship. (From 1920 to 1932, there was only one division, and the team with the best record was the champion.) Match these five teams with the number of NFL Championship Games they won during the pre–Super Bowl era from 1933 to 1965.

A. 6   Chicago Bears

B. 4   Washington Redskins

C. 3   Pittsburgh Steelers

D. 2   Philadelphia Eagles

E. 0   Detroit Lions

84. Mac's Bears were pretty invincible at Soldier Field—his last five years in Chicago, the Bears' home record (including the postseason) was 37–9; during that time, they ran off a streak of 14 straight wins. In the 1990s, a team put together a 42–3 home record over a five-year period, which included a 29-game winning streak. Their quarterback (who started every game over the five years) compiled another commendable home streak that stretched from the 1990s into the new millennium. Through 2002, his team was an undefeated 30–0 during the regular season when the game temperature was 34 degrees or less. Name the team and the quarterback.

85. Chuck Noll was head coach of one team and one team only, the Steelers, and he held that post for 23 years (1969–91), winning four Super Bowls along the way. Other coaches are prone to moving around from team to team. Here are five men who served as head coach for three different teams. (Parcells started his fourth head coaching job, with the Cowboys, in 2003.) For each, pick out the team that is *not* included among his head coaching jobs, then rank them from best to worst in career regular-season winning percentage.

Coach	Teams
Sid Gillman	Rams, Chargers, Oilers, 49ers
Forrest Gregg	Chiefs, Browns, Bengals, Packers
Chuck Knox	Vikings, Rams, Seahawks, Bills
Bill Parcells	Giants, Patriots, Raiders, Jets
Jack Pardee	Oilers, Cardinals, Bears, Redskins

86. What college has produced the most NFL players over the years, and which schools rank second and third? What about Mac's proud alma mater, Brigham Young—have they turned out many pro players? Listed below are 10 colleges, including the top three in producing NFL talent as well as BYU. Rank them from 1 (most) to 10 (least). And then go to the easier part, we think, and match the players on the right with the schools where they played college ball.

Brigham Young	Norm Van Brocklin
Notre Dame	Dan Marino
Oregon	Keyshawn Johnson
Pittsburgh	Todd Christensen
Florida	Dave Butz
Yale	Brian Piccolo
Ohio State	Emmitt Smith
Purdue	Dave Duerson
Wake Forest	Dick Jauron
USC	Pepper Johnson

87. Receiving piss-poor medical advice didn't end for Jim when he left the Bears. Late in the 1991 season, when he was with Philly, the Eagles traveled to the Meadowlands to play the Giants. The defensive line for the Giants included Leonard Marshall, Eric Dorsey, and a 6'5", 310-pound nose tackle whose only year with the Giants—and last in the NFL—was '91, after he had spent four years with the Steelers. In the second quarter, Mac was letting go of a pass and was drilled by the nose tackle. Initially, Mac thought he only had the wind knocked out of him, but he soon realized it was more serious when he had so much difficulty breathing that the game was halted for 10 minutes. Back in the locker room, the doctor looked over Mac and offered a brilliant suggestion: "Let's do an x-ray on your *shoulder*." He must have gone to the same medical school as the Bears' old doctor. In response to that suggestion, Mac snapped, "What the hell does my *shoulder* have to do with my not being able to breathe?" They gave him some pills, which did little to reduce his pain, threw him in a car, and took him to Philadelphia, where stop-and-go traffic on the New Jersey Turnpike made the trip longer. Mac was in so much pain, he was practically delirious, and he didn't hesitate to let the others in the car know that he was in a lot of discomfort. He finally made it to Philly, where, thankfully, he was treated by a doctor that wasn't a hack, who figured out what had happened—Jim had broken five ribs, and his season was over. Boy, if only that shoulder x-ray had been done, maybe Jim could have been back in uniform for the next game. Who laid the hit on Jim that prematurely ended his season in '91?

A. Jumpy Geathers

B. Frank Giannetti

C. Mark Duckens

D. Lorenzo Freeman

E. Danny Stubbs

88. Sit back and try to remember the most prolific and successful NFL head coaches ever—the real legends. All right, whom did you think of besides Frank Kush and David Shula? Seriously, of the guys you thought of, now come up with the coaches who replaced the legends after they coached their last game. Of the successors, did anybody's name pop up twice? It should have. What coach—who was very successful himself—filled the shoes of two of the NFL's all-time greatest coaches?

89. Mac will tell you that during his days with the Bears, nothing irked him more than getting sacked by some defensive lineman for a loss—except maybe being on the receiving end of an earful of crap from Ditka. Because Mac had a strong offensive line with Chicago and could scramble, he didn't get sacked much. But there was a quarterback from Mac's era whose ability to avoid sacks was uncanny. His team led the NFL in the fewest sacks allowed eight consecutive years when he was QB and also the year before he arrived for a record nine straight seasons. One of those years, his team allowed *seven* sacks the entire 16-game season. (That sometimes was a game's worth for a Buddy Ryan–

coached team.) Over a two-year stretch, they went *19* games in a row without permitting a sack. Ladies and gentleman, that's pass protection. Name the quarterback who rarely was tackled behind the line.

    A. Steve Grogan

    B. Dan Fouts

    C. Dan Marino

    D. Jim Kelly

    E. Phil Simms

90. Isn't it fun to watch the NCAA tournament in March and see some dark horses—small schools, like Gonzaga and Weber State—make it to the "Sweet 16" with Duke, UCLA, and the rest of the perennial powerhouses? At the same time, it's nice to see on NFL draft day when players get picked from small Division II or III schools. It's even better when the player goes on to star in the NFL. Here is information about four such players—you may not have heard of their colleges, but their names are definitely familiar. Who are they?

    A. Jets kickoff return specialist Bruce Harper and Cowboys reserve running back Doug Dennison played college ball in the 1970s at Kutztown University, a Division II school 75 miles northwest of Philadelphia. But neither is the best player that Kutztown has ever turned out. Kutztown alums like to brag that a guy who ranks in the top five on the NFL's all-time receptions list played football at their school.

B. For a few years in the late 1960s and early 1970s, the Minnesota Vikings' defensive front four were nicknamed "the Purple People-Eaters." The line featured Alan Page, Carl Eller, Jim Marshall, and the only NFL player to date to suit up for Concordia University located in the Chicago suburb of River Forest, Illinois. The L.A. Rams drafted him in 1964, but after a year he was traded to Minnesota, and he played a decade with the Vikings where he, along with Page, Eller, and company, made life miserable for opponents' offenses.

C. Ever heard of Yankton College? We haven't either. In fact, this school of about 600 students, located in Yankton, South Dakota, has long since closed shop, but not before this ferocious defensive end roughed up quarterbacks and running backs from 1967 to 1970. He later played 15 years for the Broncos, Browns, and Raiders. He was just 43 when he died, and his death was linked to steroid use.

D. Quarterbacks especially are known for playing in big-time college football programs—but not this guy. He was signed as a nondrafted free agent by the Seahawks in 1996 out of Central

Washington in Ellensburg, Washington, a school that has produced only a handful of NFL players. He played a season in the World League, spent some time on the Seattle bench, but then broke through as the 'Hawks starter and threw for more than 6,000 yards in 1999–2000, and cracked the 6,000 mark for another team in 2001–2002.

91. Bengals fans, this one's for you. Times have been tough lately for football followers in Cincinnati, but we're sure you're quick to remind hecklers that your boys made it to the Super Bowl twice in the 1980s, following the 1981 and 1988 seasons. The years were practically carbon copies of each other: 12–4 during the regular season, two wins in the play-offs, including one against the Bills, and then hard-fought losses to the 49ers in the Super Bowl. We counted six men who played for the Bengals both seasons. You Cincy die-hards probably can rattle them off in your sleep without any clues, but everybody else is going to need some help, so we'll fire some hints at you.

A. This tiny (5′6″, 160 pounds) place-kicker was nailing the field goals and extra points in Cincinnati for 12½ years, among the longest runs for a kicker on one team.

B. His career spanned the two Bengals Super Bowl seasons. In '81, his rookie year, he was a

big part of the offense with 67 catches and
eight touchdowns. By '88, his final year, he
was a reserve and his numbers were down to
13 and one. You've seen his face a lot in recent
years on one of the networks' pregame shows
and as a game broadcaster.

C. This left tackle wasn't just All-Pro for a season,
or All-Decade, he was *All-Century*. In 1994, a
committee of media and league personnel
chose the 75th Anniversary All-Time team,
and this 285-pound brute from USC was one
of the tackles. His plaque is on the wall in the
Hall of Fame.

D. Another offensive lineman who played college
ball in the Los Angeles area (he went to
UCLA), this excellent guard was in the
trenches for 16 years—11 with the Bengals,
followed by 5 with the Raiders.

E. His entire 14-year career (1976–89) was with
the Bengals. This Ivy Leaguer—he went to
Dartmouth—played right outside linebacker
for Cincinnati.

F. This is the most difficult of the six. A reserve
quarterback throughout his nine-year career (he
spent a year with the Falcons, the rest with the
Bengals), he threw only 504 passes—but
completed 62 percent of them. An interesting
fact about him: he also liked baseball when he

was young, and in 1968, he played in the Little League World Series against a team from Japan.

92. There is a handful of men at the helm of NFL teams in 2002 who are former teammates and/or coaches of Mac. One is the best head coach that he ever played for. Sorry, Mike D., it's not you—but you're a close second. We're counting on you to hit at least three of these.

A. He was an offensive guard/tackle for Jimmy Mac for three years at BYU. Fifteen years later, Mac signed with the Packers, and his old BYU lineman was one of the assistant offensive coaches. Upon his arrival, Mac ribbed him, "You didn't block for me then, what are you gonna show me now?" Jim was really busting chops—he thought his Packers coach was a good, scrappy lineman. He landed his first head coaching job in 1999 and, after a 5–11 debut, took his team to the play-offs the next three years.

B. The Bears drafted him out of USC in 1981. He spent four years with Chicago—three when Mac was there—as a reserve defensive back and regular punt returner before an ankle injury ended his career when he was only 26. He went into coaching soon after his retirement and was in his fifth and final year on the Eagles' staff under Buddy Ryan (first as defensive backs coach, then defensive coordinator) when Mac came to Philly in 1990. As a head coach, he came within an eyelash of winning the Super Bowl in January 2000.

C. This San Francisco native had connections with Jim at the high school, college, and pro levels. A high school team for whom he was an assistant coach from 1975 to 1980, Oak Grove High, played the team that Jim quarterbacked when he was in the ninth and tenth grades (1973–74) before his family moved to Utah. He became the quarterbacks coach of BYU in 1982, a year after Mac left, and tutored Steve Young. Later, when Mac was wrapping up his career with the Packers, this man was his head coach—the best Jim ever played for. As much as Mac enjoys needling Ditka, he thinks the guy did a hell of a job coaching the Bears. A criticism: Ditka worked the players so damn hard during the season, by the time the postseason came around they were tired, which is one of the reasons they bailed out early in the play-offs some years.

D. This Oklahoman was another Packers coach during Mac's stay in Green Bay. And he also had Oak Grove High on his resume—he played his high school ball there during the time when Mac was setting records at BYU.

He was Brett Favre and Mac's quarterbacks coach in 1996, when Green Bay won the Super Bowl. He landed his first head coaching job in 2001 when he was 39.

93. Back in the 1960s, the Bears' awesome defense, led by Dick Butkus, was nicknamed "Monsters of the Midway." Two decades later, the Cowboys were nicknamed "America's Team," and after Mac and the gang stormed into Dallas late in the 1985 season and kicked the crap out of them 44–0, Dan Hampton was asked whether it would be more appropriate for the Bears, who were 11–0, to be "America's Team." Hamp joked that, crazy sonovabitches that the Bears players were, they wouldn't want to be called "America's Team," but maybe "Kremlin's Team" would fit. Through the years, teams or parts of teams—offensive lines, defensive lines, groups of wide receivers—have been handed, usually by the media, some unique and memorable nicknames. We'll give you the nickname; you come up with the team and era. If you come up with some of the key players, that's icing on the cake.

A. "the New York Sack Exchange"

B. "the Electric Company"

C. "the Hogs"

D. "the Fun Bunch"

E. "No Name Defense"

F. "the Steel Curtain"

G. "the Fearsome Foursome"

H. "Orange Crush"

I. "Doomsday"

J. "Killer Bees"

94. If we asked you to name the career leaders in touchdowns for some teams, like the Cowboys, 49ers, Bears, and Lions, you'd scoff and say that we were insulting your football IQs. After all, you'd spit out Emmitt, Jerry, Walter, and Barry without batting an eye. So we'll make you think and see if you can come up with the touchdown leaders for a few other teams. For each, we'll give you the player's position, the number of touchdowns, and his first and last years with that team. Because a touchdown is six points, it's appropriate that we ask you for the leader of six teams, but then of course you can go for the two-point conversion as we add a pair of hard ones.

Player	Team	Position	TDs	First Year	Last Year
A.	Seattle Seahawks	Wide receiver	101	1976	1989
B.	San Diego Chargers	Wide receiver	83	1962	1970
C.	New York Giants	Running back/ wide receiver	78	1952	1964
D.	Cincinnati Bengals	Running back	70	1977	1983
E.	Philadelphia Eagles	Wide receiver	79	1971	1983
F.	Washington Redskins	Wide receiver	90	1964	1977
G.	New Orleans Saints	Running back	53	1986	1993
H.	Baltimore/Indianapolis Colts	Running back/ wide receiver	113	1956	1967

95. When Dick LeBeau replaced Bruce Coslet as the Bengals' head coach three games into the 2000 season, he became—at age 63—the oldest first-time head coach since the NFL and AFL merged in 1970. Impressive accomplishment by Dick, but we're more impressed with the number of interceptions he made as a cornerback for the Lions from 1959 through 1972: 62, which is good for a tie for sixth on the all-time list. The leader in that category picked off 81, including 12 in his rookie season and 2 in his *first game*. Can you pick out the NFL's all-time interception leader from these five defensive backs?

A. Everson Walls
B. Dick "Night Train" Lane
C. Ronnie Lott
D. Emmitt Thomas
E. Paul Krause

96. This one might get on your nerves because the format will remind you too much of a test question in school, so if you feel like skipping it, we won't be offended. Mac would have blown this one off in a second if it weren't his book. Here's the deal if you want to give it a go. We think it's quite a coincidence that three of football's best defensive backs in recent years have the same last name: Woodson—Charles, Darren, and Rod. They're unrelated, but they play like they have the same genes—each can cover, tackle, and intercept. Let's see how much you know about the Woodson boys. We'll give you eight statements, and you have to figure out if each applies to all three, some, or none of them. So answer with a 1 if it applies only to Charles; 2—only Darren; 3—only Rod; 4—Charles and Darren; 5—Darren and Rod; 6—Charles and Rod; 7—all three; 8—none of them.

A. Was picked in the first round of the NFL draft

B. Has not played for the 49ers

C. Played linebacker in college and then moved to the secondary in the pros

D. Won the Heisman Trophy

E. Has seen action in at least two Pro Bowls

F. Has played on a Super Bowl champion team

G. Is in the top 10 in career interceptions

H. Played college ball at Notre Dame

97. A 10-game winning streak for an NFL team is no easy feat—since the merger in 1970, a team has won 10 or more regular-season games in a row fewer than 25 times. The Bears hold the record with 17, which they set in the 1930s, and they won 16 straight in the 1940s. The Dolphins also ran off 16 consecutive wins, which they accomplished twice, once in their perfect 1972 season and again in 1983–84, at the beginning of the Dan Marino era. Mac's Bears won 13 consecutive games in 1984–85 and 11 straight in 1986–87. Many of the teams who compiled the streaks went on to win the Super Bowl, including the '72 Dolphins and '85 Bears. (The '84 Dolphins lost the Super Bowl.) There was a team in the '90s that didn't make it to the Super Bowl but sure had the firepower to do it. They put together an 11-game winning streak en route to a 14–2 season, scored 62 points in a divisional play-off win, but then were beaten in their conference championship game. Name the team.

A. Indianapolis Colts

B. Jacksonville Jaguars

C. Minnesota Vikings

D. Carolina Panthers

E. Houston Oilers

98. L.A. Rams fans from way back, this one is yours. We'll bet you remember well those tremendous defensive teams the Rams turned out in the 1970s. They are the only team since the 1940s (when teams played only 11 games) to allow fewer than 200 points five straight seasons (1973–77). Two of the stalwarts on that defensive unit, an end and a linebacker, have bios that are so similar, it's scary. To start off, they were born four weeks apart in 1950. The end was drafted in the first round by the Rams in 1971; two years later, the Rams picked the linebacker in the second round. The end played his entire career with the Rams, retiring in '84; the linebacker played all but half a season with the Rams and also called it quits in '84. The end stood 6′4″ and his playing weight was between 240 and 250 pounds; the linebacker was 6′3″ and usually weighed in between 235 and 240. And finally, if that's not enough, they have the same last name—and it's not a very common one—and the same first initial. Name this pair.

99. How does a coach consistently turn out good teams but then have to endure watching his boys collapse in the play-offs and get bumped in the first round? Even the brilliant minds of McMahon and Brown are at a loss for an answer. This man is one of about 25 head coaches in history with 100 or more regular-season victories. But he's the only one—at least when this book was printed—without a single postseason win. Here are some of the sad stories. In 1987, he led the NFC team he was coaching to a 12–3 record—including a 19–17 win against the Bears at Soldier Field—and a wild-card berth, then got spanked by the Vikings at home, 44–10. In 1991, his guys won the division with an 11–5 mark and led the Falcons by 10 points in the opening round of the play-offs, only to lose 27–20. By 1999, he was over in the AFC. Great team he had that year, as they cruised to a 13–3 record. But they found a way to lose to the Titans in the divisional play-off game. A year later, he came up short for the sixth straight time in postseason, as his squad pissed away a 14-point lead to the Dolphins and went down 23–17. Good thing he won a couple USFL titles in the '80s; otherwise, he'd really be beating his head against the wall. Name this hard-luck NFL coach.

100. We realize that the Super Bowl does not always live up to all the hype because too often the game is a blowout by the third quarter. (It didn't take that long for Mac's Bears to bury the Patriots.) But we're confident that you'll remember the combatants in these lopsided games. Match the teams with their opponents that they either routed or were routed by (20 or more points) in the Super Bowl.

A. Routed by Green Bay Packers   Buffalo Bills

B. Routed by Dallas Cowboys   Los Angeles Raiders

C. Routed New York Giants   Kansas City Chiefs

D. Routed Washington Redskins   San Diego Chargers

E. Routed by San Francisco 49ers   Baltimore Ravens

Slants Across the Middle

Who Am I?

101. I wore the Bears' blue and orange only for parts of two seasons, but I was extended one more invitation to Thanksgiving dinner at Mike Ditka's house than Jim was. Chicago signed me in the middle of the 1986 season when Jim was battling a shoulder injury; soon after, the coach invited my wife and me over for Turkey Day, and we gladly accepted. I saw action in four games for the Bears down the stretch, throwing 46 passes. We won the NFC Central that season, and after a bye were set to play the Redskins in the divisional play-offs. Jim's season-ending shoulder injury in November made him unavailable, and Coach Ditka had to choose among Steve Fuller, Mike Tomczak, and me. Jim thought the nod should have gone to Fuller or Tomczak because they were more experienced and I had trouble calling plays. Coach Ditka gave me the start, and the 'Skins beat us 27–13 at Soldier Field, thwarting the Bears' hopes for a Super Bowl repeat. By early the following season, I was off to New England, where I played sparingly for a couple of years. Then I headed north to Canada, where I tore up the CFL for eight years. I got the itch to play NFL ball again and signed with an AFC team in 1998 at the age of 35. Who am I?

102. When he was a "Monday Night Football" broadcaster, Dan Dierdorf used to love taking shots at me, calling me one of the dirtiest players in the NFL. Jim, who played with me three seasons in Philadelphia and one in Arizona, was inclined to agree—which is noteworthy because he didn't agree with Dierdorf very often. Mac said I would hit anything that moved. You're damn right I would. So I drilled guys after the play was over once in a while and taunted running backs and receivers on the other team. Hey, they were trying to take food off my table, and I was going to do everything I could to take their edge away. I was a safety on those tough Eagles teams coached by Buddy Ryan and Rich Kotite, playing in the same secondary with guys like Wes Hopkins and Eric Allen, who also weren't afraid to lay a hit on an opponent. Who am I?

103. NFL coaches and general managers are well aware that many games turn on the foot of their team's place-kicker, but you wouldn't know it from the way they shy away from kickers on draft day. Many of the best boomers of the late 1990s and early 2000s were not drafted by NFL teams but signed as free agents: Ryan Longwell, Mike Hollis,

Olinda Mare, Jeff Wilkins, and Mike Vanderjagt all had to look for teams on their own when they were passed up in the draft. Once in a while, though, a kicker gets plucked in a high round. Sebastián Janikowski was picked in the first round by the Raiders in 2000, the Lions selected Jason Hanson in round two of the '92 draft, and I was chosen by my team in the 1993 draft's third round after a stellar kicking career at the University of Hawaii. I made the pick worthwhile, as I have been one of the game's best from short, medium, and long. I missed an extra point my rookie season, then converted more than 300 in a row to set an NFL record. I've led my conference in PATs five times, which goes to show you how many touchdowns my team has scored. I've been an accurate field-goal kicker, too, hitting about 80 percent of my tries over the years. It's the long ones, however, that really crank up my adrenaline. I've drilled at least one 50-yarder each season through 2002 with five in '95 and '99, and overall my clip is about 60 percent from 50 yards or farther. My 51-yarder in Super Bowl XXXII is the second longest in the history of that event. I tied a 28-year-old NFL record in 1998 when I tattooed one from 63 yards out against Jacksonville. Hey, I was even pressured into punting service once, but I really botched it—my punt went a lame 17 yards. Of course, that's 16 yards longer than Joe Theismann's punt. Who am I?

104. How fast was I? Let me put it this way: I could match Deion Sanders, stride-for-stride, in a 100-yard dash, and I don't have to tell you that "Prime Time" could fly. I passed up the 1984 Olympics as a hurdler to sign as a wide receiver for the Bears, who had grabbed me in the first round of the 1983 draft. I played five years in Chicago, and sometimes my teammates used to get on me for not blocking. "I don't get paid to block," I told them nonchalantly. "You don't get paid to drop passes, either," Mac pointed out. All right, I admit it, I had hands like feet once in a while, but I caught a bunch too, and often turned my receptions into big gains. I caught 37 per year with the Bears, and my average yards-per-catch was almost 20. I spent my last six seasons in Los Angeles, which was fitting because I always aspired to be an actor. I maintained my 20-yard average for Al Davis's Raiders and snagged a career-high 50 passes in 1990. Who am I?

105. Buddy Ryan, defensive coordinator for the 1985 Bears and mastermind of the "46" defense, had about as much respect for offensive linemen as Jim did for the administration at Brigham Young. "Any fat ass can play offensive line," sneered Buddy. Funny thing was, in 1986, his first year as head coach, his Eagles broke—excuse me, *shattered*—the record for most sacks allowed by a team with 104. I guess any fat ass *can't* play offensive line. When Jim was reunited with Buddy in Arizona during the 1994 season, he kept bugging the old man to start him at quarterback, but Buddy kept going with Steve Beuerlein and Jay Schroeder. Finally, late in the season, the Cardinals were playing my Browns, and Buddy relented and gave Jim the start. I was a perennial All-Pro defensive tackle and was happy to see that the center on the other side of the line of scrimmage with the job of trying to block me was an ex–American Gladiator with hardly any NFL experience. Naturally, I had that guy for lunch and was in Jim's face the whole afternoon. Jim's sarcastic comment to Buddy after the game: "Thanks for the start." By the way, my older brother was one of Jim's teammates on the Bears. Who am I?

106. In the new millennium, I have two noteworthy sports achievements under my belt, one of which Jim also has accomplished, and one of which he hasn't but would like to. I quarterbacked a Super Bowl winner, and then I turned around in the off-season and shot a 62 in a round of golf at former quarterback Stan Humphries's tournament. Jim's best round to date is a 67. Before signing with the team that won the Super Bowl, I played six years with an NFC team, and my performance ran the gamut from downright lousy to very good. One year, I threw more than 400 passes but only 4 touchdowns and 18 interceptions. Two years later, I received an invite to the Pro Bowl after throwing 21 TDs against only 11 interceptions. I've had a little fumblitis in my career, which also plagued Jim's dear friend Randall Cunningham; Randall led the NFL in that category three times and led the NFC another season. Who am I?

107. After playing my college ball for Penn State, I was picked by the Jets in the 1978 draft and spent 12 years with them as a tight end. I played sporadically my first six years in New York, averaging only 14 catches a season, but then in 1984, I became a favorite target of quarterback Ken O'Brien and caught at least 65 passes four of the next five years. I finished my career with two years in Philly, and while I didn't see much playing time on the field, I saw plenty of practical joking orchestrated by one Jim McMahon. I remember this night during training camp in 1991 when I heard a lot of commotion in the dorm where we were staying. A couple of my Eagles teammates were sneaking up and down halls, opening doors, and spraying guys with fire extinguishers. I happened to be standing by the elevator on my floor, when I spotted the two guilty parties—McMahon and his sidekick, tackle Ron Heller. I said to them matter-of-factly, "I knew it was you two pricks." The next day, we held a team meeting (minus Mac and Hel) and decided to seek revenge. We made a pilgrimage to Kmart and cleaned them out of fire extinguishers. They sensed that we were up to something, and chicken-shits that they were, hid out in the room across the hall from Coach Rich Kotite to avoid the onslaught. Who am I?

108. Since not long after their trip to the Super Bowl following the 1988 season, the Bengals have, to be diplomatic, struggled mightily as they have posted too many 3–13 and 4–12 seasons. They had a golden opportunity to improve themselves when they had the first pick in the draft back-to-back years (which is one of the benefits of finishing 3–13). Things didn't quite work out like they hoped. In 1995, they chose running back Ki-Jana Carter out of Penn

State; he sustained a serious knee injury during his first training camp, and he never did much for the Bengals. The year before, I decided to enter the draft following my sophomore season at Ohio State, and the Bengals were impressed enough with my size (6′5″, 315 pounds; my nickname is "Big Daddy") and ability as defensive tackle (I made *The Sporting News* All-American first team in 1993) to pick me ahead of Marshall Faulk in the draft. The Bengals' brass keeps cringing as Marshall continues to crank out All-Pro seasons. As for me, I haven't been a flop, but I haven't set the world on fire, either. I'm still waiting for my first invitation to the Pro Bowl—I guess maybe if I would reach double digits in sacks in a season, they'd think about picking me. The Bengals got tired of my not living up to my potential and declined to match the offer tendered by an NFC team, and I left Cincy and flew east in 1998. My most memorable moment came with my new team in 1999 when I intercepted a pass by Bears quarterback Shane Matthews and lumbered 88 yards for a touchdown. Who am I?

109. I led Mac's 1985 Super Bowl champion Bears' team in tackles made and opinions expressed. A graduate of Yale, I had some brains and—as Jim liked to point out—I didn't mind letting people know it. My smarts helped me "quarterback" the great Bears defense that featured, among others, Steve McMichael on the line, Otis Wilson at linebacker, Dave Duerson as strong safety, and me as free safety. When I wasn't flapping my gums or burying a running back with a tackle, I was cutting in front of a receiver to pick off a pass. I totaled 38 interceptions in my 12 years in Chicago, which makes me the team's all-time interception leader. Who am I?

⬤ **110.** Jimmy Mac threw to many a receiver in his day, but he rated me as the cream of the crop. We were teammates on the Eagles my last two years in the league, and by that time I was past my prime and was a backup to Calvin Williams and Fred Barnett. At the top of my game with the Cardinals, though, I put up some impressive numbers. In 1983, I rolled up 1,227 yards in the air and scored 14 touchdowns, including 4 in *one half* against the Seahawks. The next year, I pulled in a dozen TDs and accumulated 1,555 yards receiving. Two of the guys who deserved a lot of the credit for my success as a Cardinal were quarterback Neil Lomax, who could really thread the needle, and Ottis Anderson, who was a huge threat in the backfield that the defense always had to watch closely. Two final notes: in 1979, my rookie year, when I played primarily as a defensive back, I tied an NFL record by fielding a kickoff 6 yards deep in the end zone and galloping 106 yards for a touchdown. In 1981, I accomplished the feat of making an interception and catching a touchdown pass—in the same game. Who am I?

⬤ **111.** I was the first player chosen in the college draft by the Carolina Panthers prior to their inaugural season. It was the spring of 1995, and I was coming off a strong career as Penn State's quarterback; senior year, I was a finalist for the Heisman Trophy and led the Nittany Lions to an undefeated 12–0 record—the highlight was a victory over Oregon in the Rose Bowl. By the way, the summer after my junior year, baseball's Toronto Blue Jays drafted me, but I declined to sign, as I had when the Detroit Tigers picked me in the draft four years earlier. Things were up and down for me in Carolina—I threw too many interceptions in '95 and '97 but was consistent and led the Panthers, coached by Dom Capers, to the NFC Championship Game in '96. Another down year for me was 1998, and in the middle of the season, the Panthers waived me; I played the rest of the year for Mike Ditka's Saints. I signed with another team in the off-season and had a respectable year for them in '99, but the best was yet to come. In 2000, we weren't expected to do much, but we won our division, beat the Eagles in the divisional play-offs, and crushed the Vikings, 41–0, in the championship game on the strength of my five touchdown tosses. Mac wasn't shedding any tears when Dennis Green got his butt kicked. I didn't have it in the big game in Tampa, as I threw four interceptions, but it still felt great to go to the Super Bowl, especially considering that I had been battling some off-the-field problems—for quite a while there, I was doing too many 12-ounce curls. Who am I?

112. In the mid-1980s, the football coach at Elmer Meyers High School in the industrial town of Wilkes-Barre, Pennsylvania, had quite a luxury. He had not one, but two running backs who would star in the NFL. My brother, with his blazing speed, was halfback, and the coach made me full-back because I was the only guy on the team fast enough to block for him. We both made the move to wide receiver in college and began our NFL careers in 1993. (My brother played two years in the CFL first.) I broke in with the Vikings, and my rookie year, mainly because I was a nervous rookie, the reliable hands that I had in college deserted me. As my quarterback Jim McMahon joked, I "couldn't catch a cold" that year. In between my drops, I did make 19 catches, including a touchdown reception from Mac late in the season against the Packers. I regained my sure-handedness the following year, and my numbers improved considerably. My best days were to follow, though. For the Ravens in 1999, I cracked the 1,000-yard barrier, and in a game against the Steelers, I piled up 258 yards receiving—11th best ever. In 2000, I caught 49 passes and 5 touchdowns during the regular season and 9 more in the postseason, most notably a 44-yarder in our Super Bowl victory. I made a career-high 74 grabs in 2001. Who am I?

● 113. Augustana College is a Division III school in Rock Island, Illinois, with a student population of about 2,200. It has produced two NFL players: George Lenc, who played two games for the Brooklyn Dodgers in 1939, and me. I lasted a whole lot longer than old George—I spent 16 years as quarterback for the Bengals. I had the league's highest passing rating four seasons, twice in the 1970s and twice in the 1980s, including 1981 when I was at the top of my game. The year before, I had an off season, and in '81 I got off to a slow start and heard some boos from the Cincy fans. But then, I bore down and got very hot, leading the Bengals to a 12–4 record and the Central Division title, tossing 29 touchdowns along the way. We beat the Bills and Chargers in the play-offs but lost a tight one to the 49ers in the Super Bowl, 26–21; I threw a pair of TDs and ran for one in the losing cause. I concluded the year on another high note by winning the MVP. The next year, in the strike-shortened season, I set the NFL record for highest completion percentage with 70.6. Who am I?

114. New England drafted Drew Bledsoe first overall in the 1993 draft, and 218 picks later, San Francisco grabbed me. My rookie year was what you would expect from a 219th-round pick: as the 49ers' third-string quarterback, I didn't take a snap the whole year. My number was finally called in '94, as well as in '95 and '96, and I came through—I completed a sizzling 66 percent of my passes and threw 18 touchdowns in my part-time role. I saw the opportunity to become a starter and signed with an AFC team with whom I was number one man most of my four years there. I stunk in '98 and spent a few games warming the bench, but I was sharp the other three years, especially 2000 when I threw for 4,169 yards (third best in the league) and 28 touchdowns (fourth highest in the league). I made history in a game against the Raiders that year when I became the eighth quarterback ever to pass for more than 500 yards in a game. Get this, though—we lost the game by 18 points. I capped off the 2000 season by playing in the Pro Bowl, which wasn't my first bowl game experience—I led the Michigan Wolverines to Gator Bowl and Rose Bowl victories in college. My favorite receiver was Desmond Howard, who was also a high school teammate of mine in Cleveland. A final hint: I'm of Croatian descent—my parents came over from Croatia in 1970 and could not speak a lick of English. Who am I?

115. Jimmy Mac doesn't make any bones about it: his year with the Chargers in 1989, he thought Dan Henning's offensive system sucked. Henning called all the plays, and Mac was not allowed to audible except to throw dump-off screen passes. Mac's exasperated response: "You traded for me for *this*?!" Mac didn't find fault with one aspect of the game plan: there were a lot of passing plays to me. I caught 75 passes for San Diego that year, netting 1,252 yards and finding the end zone 10 times. I continued to be the "go-to" guy my next four years in San Diego, as I led owner Alex Spanos's team in yards receiving each year and in '93 caught a career-high 84 passes. I went the free-agency route and signed with Denver and kept up the good work for the Broncos with my fourth and fifth 1,000-yard seasons; in '95, I broke the franchise record with 14 six-point receptions. But for some reason, I was destined not to play in a Super Bowl. The year after I left the Chargers as a free agent following the '93 season, they made the Super Bowl. After my strong three seasons in Denver, I left and the Broncos won it all the next two years. And by the time I got to the Cowboys in '97, their best days were behind them—they had won the big prize three of the previous five years. So when it was all said and done, I didn't have any Super Bowl rings on my fingers, but I racked up some excellent career numbers: 595 catches, 9,148 yards, and 63 touchdowns. Who am I?

116. When the day finally comes that I have to hang up my football cleats, I'll be sad. But at least I have enough other interests and talents that I can turn to in case I want to pursue a second career: karate instructor (I'm a first-degree black belt); fisherman (I can catch bass with the best of them—I recently won a $25,000 first prize in Mississippi); and comedian (my teammates will tell you that I'm one of the funniest guys in the locker room). The way my career is going, though, my retirement may not be for a while. I've been playing linebacker for the same team since 1991 (at least through 2002), and while I was good early in my career, I got better with experience—I was All-Pro in 1998, 1999, and 2000. I recorded a bunch of sacks—especially for a linebacker—and am second to Kyle Clifton on my team's all-time tackles list. (The stat has been kept since 1976.) In 2000, I added another feather in my cap: I *ran* the ball for a first down on a fake punt. Before the pros, I played high school ball at J. C. Murray High in Atlanta (the same high school where Mac's teammate on the Bears, Richard

Dent, got his start dropping quarterbacks and running backs) and college ball at the University of Georgia, where I was All-SEC my senior year. Who am I?

🏈 **117.** I was Brigham Young's starting quarterback Mac's first two years there, and I was about as passive as he was outspoken. We had this loud-mouthed assistant coach, Wally English, who thrived on chewing out players during scrimmages. I would usually let Wally's bullshit roll off my sleeve, but Mac sometimes didn't have my restraint. This one scrimmage, a play was designed for Mac to throw to the tight end. Mac rolled out, and because the tight end wasn't open, he threw to the wide receiver who was in the clear. Wally, sounding like Ditka, screamed at Jim for not throwing to the tight end. Luckily, Wally was hard of hearing, so when Mac called him a fucking idiot, he didn't hear it. Mac thought I was a damn good quarterback but could have used a little more fire. He was probably right, although I had a good career at BYU and was drafted in the first round by the Raiders in 1980. I spent eight years playing for Al Davis, and despite some inconsistency, I held my own, as I threw for 2,000 yards four seasons and picked up a pair of Super Bowl rings. I finished up with two seasons in New England. Who am I?

🏈 **118.** I've been able to run the 40-yard dash in 5.2 seconds, which isn't world-class, but it's damn quick for a guy that's 6'7", 320 pounds. My speed, size, and strength helped me become a consensus first-team All-American offensive tackle my senior year at USC in 1994. In the college draft the following spring, the Jaguars had a difficult and important decision: whom to pick with the second overall choice. The field was impressive: quarterbacks Steve McNair and Kerry Collins; running backs Tyrone Wheatley and Napoleon Kaufman; wide receivers Joey Galloway and Michael Westbrook; and defensive linemen Kevin Carter, Warren Sapp, and Hugh Douglas, to name a few. But the Jags picked me over and above all that other talent and I didn't disappoint them. In my seven years in Jacksonville, I was regularly voted to play in the Pro Bowl, and why not? On the average, I allowed a mere 2½ sacks per season. One of my best performances came in the 1996 wild-card game against Buffalo—I held future Hall of Fame sack artist Bruce Smith to three tackles and no sacks, earning the game ball, as we beat the Bills, 30–27, at Rich Stadium. What's my greatest accomplishment, though? Marrying my wife, Angi, a former Miss California. Who am I?

119. On game day, Ditka may have ranted, raved, spat, cursed, and kicked dirt, but one thing Mac doesn't remember him doing is punching out an opposing player on the sidelines, which my coach Woody Hayes did at Ohio State. A Clemson player intercepted a pass and was tackled out-of-bounds in the vicinity of the Ohio State bench. Woody went ballistic and popped him—hell of a punch for a man in his sixties. He had quite a temper, old Woody, but the way I played for him, he didn't have any reason to drill me. I won the Heisman Trophy my junior *and* senior years for the Buckeyes (1974–75) and am the only man to date with two Heismans in his trophy case. Many pro scouts said that at 5'9", 190 pounds, I wasn't big enough to be a dominating running back in the NFL. I hate to say it, but they were right. While I wasn't a flop, I definitely was not a star. I played seven years for the Bengals, and my top yardage mark on the ground for a season was 688, in 1979. Over my career, I ran for 2,808 yards, which was OK, but then again Eric Dickerson used to do that in a season and a half. I also had this tendency *not* to score touchdowns. I ran for three my rookie year and four my last two years, but the four seasons in between, during which I ran the ball almost 500 times, not once did the official raise his arms signaling a touchdown. Same story on the receiving side: I caught 192 passes but just six for touchdowns. Who am I?

120. Since the Steelers' run of Super Bowl wins in the 1970s, they have been back to the big event only once, following the 1995 season. I was one of the big guns on Bill Cowher's team that year as I broke the team record with 85 catches, which is really saying something considering the likes of Lynn Swann and John Stallworth had long careers in Pittsburgh, and those guys could really catch the football. (Hines Ward later broke the record.) I also gained 1,307 yards in that 1995 season, but I outdid that two years later with 1,398, breaking Stallworth's Steelers record for most yards in a season. I signed with another AFC team after the

'97 season and my team made it to the Super Bowl my second year, although I missed the game due to an ankle injury. Chargers fans may remember your team drafted me in 1991. Mac's old coach Dan Henning cut me at the end of preseason, re-signed me soon after only to waive me after I played in one game without a catch, then signed me *again* that season. I appeared in three more games but did not make a reception. I was invited back to training camp in '92, by which time Bobby Ross had replaced Henning. I must have been a masochist because I went, and lightning struck again as they cut me a third time at the end of preseason. My final numbers for the Chargers: four games, zero catches, released three times. Fortunately, the Steelers and Bill Cowher gave me my chance. Who am I?

121. I've made my living trying to shake loose from 325-pound offensive linemen such as David Dixon, Earl Dotson, and James "Big Cat" Williams and stop running backs cold as well as sack quarterbacks, which is my real passion. I bounced between tackle and end my first four years, but my team moved me to end for good in 1996, and that's when I started to crank up the sacks. I was in double digits four straight years, with a high of 15 in 1999. I might have made it five in a row in 2000, except a contract squabble with my team distracted me. I got back on track with 11 drops of the QB in 2001, and in fact from 1996 through 2001, my 60 sacks trailed only Michael Strahan among NFL defenders. As good as I have been and as much notoriety as I've gotten in the NFL, I wasn't that big-time in college or high school. I played not Division I ball but Division I-AA for two colleges: Tennessee State and then South Carolina State. And I was afraid to tell Mac, but at Cainhoy High in Wando, South Carolina, I didn't letter in football until my senior year because I was concentrating on *academics*. I earned Mac's respect when I told him that I participate in some off-season celebrity golf outings. And finally, to show my goodwill, a teammate of mine for many years, Tracy Scroggins, and I helped a local nonprofit organization called "Focus: Hope" by donating 250 turkeys to the underprivileged on Thanksgiving. Many of the recipients over the years have eaten those turkeys while watching Tracy and me play on Thanksgiving. Who am I?

122. My trademarks were a North Carolina drawl, a little paunch, and an incredible knack for pulling out games in the fourth quarter by marching my team down the field with some sweetly thrown passes. Among quarterbacks who started their careers before 1970, I rank third in touchdown passes with 255 and fifth in passing yards with 32,000 and change. In my first four years in the league with the Eagles, I went crazy sitting on the bench most of the time as future Hall of Famer Norm Van Brocklin ran the show. When "the Dutchman" retired after the '60 season in which he led Philadelphia to the NFL championship, I finally got my shot—and didn't blow it. I led the league in passing yards two straight years and touchdown tosses once. The Birds traded me (for Norm Snead) to Washington after the 1963 season, and I picked up where I left off with Philly, leading the NFL in yards in the air three more seasons and touchdowns once. One of the years that I topped the league in yards, 1966, I played in a record-setting game; my Redskins scored 72 points—a record for a team in a regular-season game. We scored 10 touchdowns, and I threw three of them. It's a good thing we had the offense in extra high gear because the Giants scored 41 points that day. By the way, our 72 points was one shy of the record 73 that the Bears scored against the Redskins in the 1940 Championship Game. What makes it so unbelievable that the Redskins allowed so many points is they gave up an average of only 13 a game during the season. To add insult to injury, Washington was blanked that day, so the final score was 73–0. We have watched some bad Super Bowls, but nothing like that. Back to my career. I played less and less as I got into my late thirties, but I still had the touch. In my last year, 1974, at age 40, wily veteran that I was, I completed 64 percent of my passes and chucked 11 touchdowns in only 167 throws. Who am I?

123. Along with linebackers Tom Jackson and Karl Mecklenburg and defensive backs Dennis Smith and Louis Wright, I was one of the forces on those excellent Broncos defenses in the 1980s, early in John Elway's career. I was voted All-Pro at defensive end three times, largely because of my penchant for dropping the quarterback—I averaged 10½ sacks per year from 1984 through 1987; my high was 13½ in '86. I almost sacked the elusive Jim McMahon early in the 1984 season and inadvertently injured him in the process. We were at Solider Field the second week of the season, and in the first quarter, Jim was in the pocket looking downfield. I slipped past my man, was bearing down on Jim for a sack, and drilled him just before he delivered a pass for a touchdown. When I came down on Jim, I accidentally landed on his throwing hand. The Bears' team doctor took a look and said it was a minor injury—only a bruise. That night, Jim was eating dinner with tight end Jay Saldi and had problems cutting his steak. He decided to seek an opinion from a competent doctor and learned to his chagrin that he'd actually suffered a hairline fracture of the right hand. Jim got injections to his hand and wore a cast on it at night, but he continued to practice during the day and play on Sundays—and effectively. He had the highest quarterback rating (97.8) in a season for his career, but then he suffered the lacerated kidney a few weeks later, which knocked him out for the season. One last clue: I grew up and went to high school in Ogden, Utah, just a few miles from Roy, where Jim spent the second half of high school. Who am I?

124. I'm not bullshitting—here is the story of how I made it to the NFL. I grew up in Australia and played seven years in the Australian Rules Football League. In 1994, I won two round-trip plane tickets in a long-ball-kicking contest and, because I was about to get married, decided to use the tickets for my honeymoon to Los Angeles with my soon-to-be wife, Rosemary. She had told me the one thing, above all, that she wanted to do on our honeymoon was watch me kick, so while we were there we took a ride down to San Diego so

I could participate in a punting tryout with the Chargers. Things got off to a rocky start—I really had the butterflies— and the first snap from the long snapper drilled me in the schnoz. While Rosemary was cracking up, I regained my composure and impressed Chargers general manager Bobby Beathard enough with my punts that he made me an offer. I spent the '94 season on the practice squad, while Bryan Wagner was the team's regular punter. But the following training camp, I won the job—and made the Pro Bowl by finishing second in the league with a 44.7 average. I've kept booming the ball since, always finishing among the league's top punters. In 2000, I had an especially good year, as I led the NFL with a 46.2 average, earning an invitation back to the Pro Bowl. I give a lot of credit to my long snapper of many years, David Binn. His snaps are always right on the money—not one time in eight years has he hit me in the nose. I was so appreciative, I picked up the tab for Dave and his girlfriend, Tamar, to travel to Hawaii with Rosemary, our son, and me for the Pro Bowl following the 2000 season. It's been fun playing in the states, but I haven't forgotten my Australian roots. I still spend time in Melbourne in the off-season and respond to fans' questions about Australian football via E-mail. Who am I?

125. You don't hear the NFL's talking heads singing my praises the way they have Jerry Rice, Randy Moss, and Isaac Bruce, but ask any cornerback in the league and he'll tell you it's no picnic trying to cover me—or catch me once I make a reception. Early in my career, for the Ravens in '96 and '97, I had back-to-back 60-reception, 1,000-yard, nine-touchdown seasons. But I really got down to business in 2000 for the Chiefs when I hauled in 78 passes for almost 1,400 yards. The big gainer is my forte. As great as Cris Carter has been, he hasn't had a pass reception of more than 80 yards; I've had *six* through 2002, and I added another 80-yarder on a reverse play. My family has had more than its share of tragedy, which has driven me to play hard every game. One of my brothers, Garrett, died in 1996, and I dedicated that season with the Ravens to him. The same year, I switched my uniform number to 82, which another deceased brother, Steven, wore as a high school player. The losses of Garrett and Steven have been really tough on my family, but it's brought us closer and made us more supportive of each other. In fact, my parents have attended every one of my home games in the NFL, at the University of Michigan, and at Benedictine High School in Detroit. And on a lighter note, I appeared on "Wheel of Fortune" during NFL players' week prior to the Super Bowl in 1999 and beat out Curtis Conway and Wesley Walls in the championship round. It was good to meet Pat and Vanna, and also to win almost $40,000, which I put toward a foundation that I opened to benefit grieving children and their families. Who am I?

Mixed Bag

🏈 **126.** We know that as a player, Jim was colorful and controversial, but what about as a kid? Was he a studious geek or a rebellious troublemaker? Here are 10 true-or-false statements about Jim's younger years.

A. The first time Jim was sent to the principal's office was in his fourth week of kindergarten.

B. Little Jim was a diligent student who enthusiastically did his homework every night and as a result consistently got straight A's.

C. Jim was mild-mannered in elementary school, and whenever there was an opportunity for a fight, he turned it down.

D. At all times, Jim treated his teachers with the utmost respect.

E. When Jim was 12, some of the kids in his neighborhood asked him if he wanted to try smoking, but he told them he didn't because it was bad for his health.

F. His favorite sport growing up was football, and it wasn't until his adulthood that he switched to golf.

G. In junior high, he broke into his school and marked up the walls with graffiti.

H. At his high school, if a student got three pink slips for cutting class, fighting, etc., he was supposed to get suspended; Jim stayed under the limit and avoided suspension.

I. Jim's father was pleased with his exemplary behavior in high school and bought him a car for his 16th birthday.

J. When the guys in Jim's dorm freshman year in college were making too much noise late at night, he would come out of his room and politely ask them to keep the noise down.

127. You became so accustomed to seeing John Elway wear his Broncos uniform, you may have forgotten that he was drafted by another NFL team. He made it clear prior to the draft in 1983 that he wouldn't play for them, so they were forced to trade him and dealt the future Hall of Famer to the Broncos shortly after the draft. Likewise, it is hard to picture three-time Associated Press MVP Brett Favre playing for anybody but the Packers, but actually another team picked him up in the 1991 draft. He appeared in only two games for them in '91, throwing five passes with no completions and two interceptions, and was dealt to Green Bay after the season. Go ahead and match Elway, Favre, and three other excellent quarterbacks with the teams that drafted them but for whom they played little or not at all.

A. Tampa Bay Buccaneers   Mark Brunell

B. Baltimore Colts   Jim Everett

C. Atlanta Falcons   John Elway

D. Houston Oilers   Brett Favre

E. Green Bay Packers   Steve Young

128. Baseball players don't take the beating that football players do, so it is not surprising that while dozens of men have played 20 or more years on the major league diamond, through 2002 a mere seven have lasted two decades on the NFL gridiron. Two were well-traveled quarterbacks from a generation ago. One also handled his team's place-kicking duties; the other was Bob Griese's backup on the Dolphins 1972 team that went undefeated. Two others played on the line, one defensive and one offensive. The defensive player started his career with the Browns but played his remaining 19 years for another team. The offensive lineman spent his entire career with the same team, although they moved to a different city in 1995 for his last year in the league. The other three were still playing in 2002, so you probably don't need us to tell you anything about their positions or teams. Name the seven players as well as the teams they played for.

129. Quarterbacks and running backs steal most of the headlines after Super Bowls, but place-kickers have made their mark in football's biggest event. Think back and see how many of these kickers you can remember from Super Bowls past.

A. This strong-footed, soccer-style Norwegian got the Chiefs off to a 9–0 start by kicking three first-half field goals, and they rolled to a 23–7 win over the Vikings in Super Bowl IV in January 1970.

B. With five seconds left in Super Bowl V, what Colts rookie kicker made a 32-yard field goal to break a 13–13 tie and beat the Cowboys in their first of many Super Bowls?

C. This booter helped the Steelers and Giants win Super Bowls, while his brother contributed three field goals and eight extra points to the Raiders' two victories in the 1980s.

D. Name the kicker from Jim's Bears team who connected for three field goals and tacked on five extra points in their 46–10 whipping of the Patriots. Jim told Brown not to forget to mention that this man went on to set many Bears kicking records, including most career field goals and extra points and most field goals in a season.

E. The Bills lost four straight Super Bowls in the early 1990s, and the first of those against the Giants following the 1990 season was the closest they came to winning. It was nip-and-tuck throughout the game, and with time running out and the Giants clinging to a 20–19 lead, what kicker's 47-yard field goal sailed wide right, as the Bills and their fans suffered a heartbreaking loss?

130. With Jim and Walter Payton leading the offensive attack and Mike Singletary and Dan Hampton spearheading the defense, the 1985 Bears were practically perfect as they rolled up 15 wins during the regular season, losing only to the Dolphins on Monday night in the 13th week. Since the NFL lengthened the schedule from 14 to 16 games in 1978, only two other teams through 2002 have posted 15–1 records. One accomplished the feat in the 1980s and went on to win the Super Bowl, beating the Bears in the NFC Championship Game to get there; the other team went 15–1 in the 1990s but was denied a trip to the big game when they lost the NFC Championship Game to the Falcons in overtime. Name these terrific teams.

131. There have been several NFL players with blood ties to athletes in other sports, including baseball, basketball, and golf. Match these active or recently retired football players with their relatives who have excelled in other sports.

A.	Cousin of well-traveled NBA forward Sam Perkins	Bobby Taylor
B.	Son of gold-medal member of 400-meter relay team at 1972 Summer Olympics	Rodney Peete
C.	Cousin of NHL/WHA player from the 1970s and 1980s, Mike Rogers, who was a teammate of Wayne Gretzky's	Eddie Murray
D.	Nephew of Jim "Mudcat" Grant, major league pitcher who won 145 games	Thomas Smith
E.	Cousin of longtime professional golfer	Darren Hambrick

132. Wait a minute here! Jim McMahon's name keeps cropping up in a lot of these questions, so why do we hardly ever see the name of his counterpart Dave Brown? He worked hard on this book, too. While Mac is the only Jim McMahon so far who has played in the NFL, there have been four Dave Browns to grace the gridiron. (The coauthor is most definitely *not* one of them; the scouting report on him as a backyard football player was grim: poor hands, a shoddy tackler, runs the 40 in seven flat.) We're looking for the teams for whom the namesakes of the coauthor played.

A. The first Dave Brown was a reserve running back for three years for this team in the 1940s. It's probably not much of a hint that one of his teammates, Bill Paschal, led the league in rushing in 1943 and another, Mel Hein, was a college professor during the week and played center on Sundays. You think Ditka would tolerate that?

B. D.B. number two could really play. He's in the top 10 on the all-time interception list with 62; 50 of the picks were for this AFC team from 1976 until 1986.

C. His NFL career was rather abbreviated: just one game at linebacker as a replacement player during the 1987 strike. The regular linebackers on his team included Byron Evans, Garry Cobb, and Mike Reichenbach.

D. After three years as the starter and one year as a part-timer for the Giants in the mid-1990s, this D.B., a mediocre quarterback, signed with another team in 1998, where he continued his mediocrity as a backup.

133. What a potent tandem Jim Kelly and Andre Reed were for the Bills. From the mid-1980s to the mid-1990s, Kelly was consistently one of the NFL's most efficient quarterbacks, thanks much in part to Reed, who regularly finished among the league leaders in receptions. They helped the Bills win four straight AFC championships. But do they have the most touchdown connections of any quarterback-to-receiver combination in NFL history—or is it one of the four other pairs listed below?

A. Jim Kelly to Andre Reed
B. Dan Marino to Mark Clayton
C. Troy Aikman to Michael Irvin
D. Johnny Unitas to Raymond Berry
E. Steve Young to Jerry Rice

134. Man, did Jim hate this guy. It was Week 12 of the 1986 season, and the Bears were hosting their archrival, the Packers. Green Bay's obnoxious, loud-mouthed head coach, Forrest Gregg, was taunting Jim before the game with garbage like, "We'll get you, you bastard!" The thug that Gregg assigned the job of taking Jim out of the game was this buffoon, who claimed to play the position of nose tackle. He was so intent on carrying out the mission, he had a towel tucked inside his pants with the uniform numbers of Bears players he intended to knock out. His list of five players included Jim (No. 9), wide receiver Dennis Gentry (No. 29), and Walter Payton (No. 34). Bad enough he had his sights set on Mac and three other guys, but to target Walter, one of the classiest guys ever to play the game, was absolutely despicable. Jim already had a bad right shoulder from an injury earlier in the season, and then in the second quarter, after a play was clearly over, this imbecile body-slammed Jim on his bad shoulder, ending his season and requiring him to undergo surgery. The referee naturally tossed him out of the game, but the league slapped him on the wrist with a two-game suspension. The football gods made sure he got what he deserved, though. Two years later, after short stays with the Oilers and Falcons, his career was over. Can you name this world-class bum?

135. When the knucklehead just mentioned body-slammed Jim, he made sure to dump him on his right shoulder because Mac was a right-handed thrower. But when Jim's man "The Wild Thing" was striking out, walking, or hitting batters with his heat, he was throwing with his left arm. Left-handed pitchers are somewhat commonplace (about a quarter of big-league hurlers are southpaws), but left-handed quarterbacks are a rarity—fewer than 10 percent of NFL quarterbacks through the decades have been lefties. Here are 10 quarterbacks, 5 left-handed and 5 right-handed. Tell us who are the lefties and who are the righties. Then try to arrange them from oldest to youngest. We'll give each one's year of birth in the Answers.

Bernie Kosar	Mark Brunell
Scott Mitchell	Boomer Esiason
Ken Stabler	Mark Malone
Daunte Culpepper	Jim Zorn
Warren Moon	Charlie Batch

136. Let's go back three decades to the 1970s, when the running game was more in style than the passing game was. Here are the starting running backs for 10 different teams in 10 different years back when Mac and Brown were watching pro football on the tube. You tell us the teams for whom these guys were toting the ball.

Team	Year	Halfback	Fullback
A.	1970	Larry Brown	Charlie Harraway
B.	1971	Ed Podolak	Wendell Hayes
C.	1972	Altie Taylor	Steve Owens
D.	1973	Mike Garrett	Cid Edwards
E.	1974	Tom Sullivan	Norm Bulaich
F.	1975	Chuck Foreman	Ed Marinaro
G.	1976	Don Calhoun	Sam Cunningham
H.	1977	Anthony Davis	Ricky Bell
I.	1978	Greg Pruitt	Mike Pruitt
J.	1979	Tony Dorsett	Robert Newhouse

137. Some men have coached for an eternity in the NFL and never won a Super Bowl. On the other hand, two men were spoiled quickly, as they won it all in their maiden voyage as head coach. The first replaced Don Shula as the

Baltimore Colts' coach in 1970 and led Johnny Unitas and the boys to the top of the football world that season. Less than two years later, he was gone—short-fused general manager Joe Thomas canned him after the Colts began the '72 season 1–4. He coached the Lions to a 6–7–1 record in 1973 and died of a heart attack during training camp the following year. The second man inherited a team (which he had worked for years earlier as an usher at games) that was the defending Super Bowl champion, and they made it two in a row by winning the big game in January 1990. He became the quickest coach to win 50, 75, and 100 games. He was about as laid back on the sidelines as Ditka was intense, and he's on the eccentric side. After all, how many people do you know whose college major was zoology?

◖▦▶ 138. It may have been the most sensational two-game performance by a running back—or any player, for that matter—in college football history. In the first game, he ran for 318 yards and six touchdowns. He followed that up the week after with 350 yards but managed only five TDs. His two-game stats: 668 yards on the ground and 11 six-pointers. Those numbers aren't bad for a *season*. What active NFL running back put together those mind-numbing numbers?

A. Tyrone Wheatley
B. Ricky Williams
C. Lamar Smith
D. James Stewart
E. Mike Anderson

🏈 **139.** As the old expression goes, tying a game is like kissing your sister. The same can be said about a team finishing runner-up in its conference. Let's face it, remembering which teams have lost in Super Bowls past is a breeze, but recalling who has come out on the short end of the stick in conference championship games is difficult. Here are a few questions about teams who have lost conference championship games—and not lost them—since the NFL split into two conferences in 1970.

A. Which AFC team lost the championship game five of the first eight years under the new system established in 1970, and the last two AFL Championship Games, and thus was one win away from the Super Bowl seven times in a 10-year period? They haven't always been denied the opportunity to play for football's biggest prize—they have made it to five Super Bowls, winning three.

B. Which AFC team lost the conference championship game to Denver following the 1986, 1987, and 1989 seasons?

C. Through 2002, what franchises have won the Super Bowl but have not lost a conference championship game?

D. A NFC team set an all-time NFL record in the 1970s by winning seven straight division titles. But they were snakebit in the postseason, losing four championship games in five years (and scoring only 30 points in the four losses), and when they finally made it to the Super Bowl following the 1979 season, the Steelers beat them.

E. Two current teams (besides the Houston Texans) have neither won nor lost a championship game. Who are they?

140. In the Raiders' storied history spanning more than four decades, dating back to the AFL years, 12 different quarterbacks have led the team in passing yards for a season. One man led Al Davis's squad seven straight seasons, while another led them six years running. Of the dozen, seven took them to postseason play at least once. You Raiders' fans should clean up on this one, but even you folks who aren't supporters of the black and silver ought to be able to identify half of these quarterbacks.

141. Thirteen years before the Dolphins spoiled the Bears' chance for an undefeated season, Don Shula's '72 team, when the schedule was 14 games, went undefeated during the regular season and then rattled off three wins in the postseason for a perfect 17–0 record. Here are statements about four of the unsung stars from the 1972 World Champion Dolphins. Name them.

A. As daring as Mac could be, one thing he didn't try was wrestling alligators. He probably would have if he were sure the alligator was willing to team up with him against Ditka later on. One of the Dolphins' defensive tackles, so the story goes, actually did tangle with alligators as an off-season hobby. He tried fishing and golf, but they weren't exciting enough for him. He played his entire eight-year career with Miami.

B. The anchor of the Dolphins' offensive line, this Bethune Cookman graduate came over from the Chargers in a 1969 trade and spent a dozen years opening holes for Miami's running backs and protecting the quarterback, mainly Bob Griese. He was inducted into the Hall of Fame in 1993.

C. Larry Csonka was the Dolphins running back who got most of the ink, but this guy was *fast*. He ran for 1,000 yards on the nose in the '72 season and a league-leading 12 touchdowns. His career rushing average of 5.1 is second only to Jim Brown among backs with 750 or more attempts. In addition to being fast on the football field, he also played fast and loose with the law after he retired and ended up in the joint for a few years.

D. Paul Warfield was one of the starting wide receivers on the '72 Dolphins, and he was almost as fast as the running back we were just talking about. This guy was the other starting wide receiver, and he was very slow. "When you're as slow as I am, you don't lose any steps as you grow older," he once joked. "Monday

Night Football" broadcaster Alex Karras cracked that he "ran the 100-yard dash in 14 days." But the man had great moves and hands as well as guts and lasted 11 years with the Dolphins. He caught 212 passes and 23 touchdowns.

142. Mac played with a few hundred teammates during his 15-year NFL career. Most of them were good guys, but there were a few candy-assed punks also. He was teammates with some guys for as long as seven years, such as fellow Bears Jay Hilgenberg and Dennis Gentry. Other guys, he spent his Sundays with for only a season or part of a season. Four of those players are listed here, along with one man who never was teammates with Jimmy Mac. Name the guy Jim never played with.

A. Sean Salisbury

B. Eugene Robinson

C. Mark Herrmann

D. Pat Beach

E. Chris Bahr

143. Take a look at the list of NFL players whom the Associated Press has voted MVP since the inception of the award in 1957, and you'll see names of some of the all-time greats: Jim Brown, Jim Taylor, and Brett Favre, to name a few. Mixed in there are some guys who were good, but if you saw their names on the list, you might say, "*They* won the MVP?" They did, though. We'll give you the year, team, and position; you do the rest.

Player	Year	Team	Position
A.	1969	Los Angeles Rams	Quarterback
B.	1972	Washington Redskins	Running back
C.	1976	Baltimore Colts	Quarterback
D.	1980	Cleveland Browns	Quarterback
E.	1982	Washington Redskins	Kicker

🏈 **144.** We've watched some Super Bowls that went down to the wire, but we're still waiting for one that ends in a tie after regulation and goes into overtime. Eight years before the first Super Bowl, on December 28, 1958, the Colts and Giants squared off in the NFL Championship Game, which did go into overtime. Colts quarterback Johnny Unitas was the hero as he orchestrated two long drives, one late in the fourth quarter that culminated in the game-tying field goal, and one in overtime that led to the game-winning touchdown. The final was 23–17, and some have hailed it as "the greatest game ever played." Here are four questions about that classic battle almost half a century ago. If you're like Mac and Brown and weren't even born when the game was played, try picking the brain of some of your older relatives.

A. Who opened up the scoring with a 36-yard field goal for the Giants in the first quarter and later kicked two extra points? His longtime broadcasting partner was an outstanding coach in the 1970s before going upstairs to the booth.

B. Who was the Giants' quarterback, who had held the job for 11 years, who tossed a touchdown pass to Frank Gifford in the fourth quarter to put New York ahead, 17–14?

C. What burly Colts running back, nicknamed "the Horse," barreled in from the 1-yard line in overtime to win the game?

D. Who was the victorious head coach of the Colts that day? He beat his old team in the Super Bowl a decade later.

145. In the first seven years of the AFL, 1960–66, the NFL and AFL held separate drafts, so many players were picked by a team in each league. While there were exceptions, like Joe Namath and Fred Biletnikoff, most of the marquee players signed with a team from the more established and prestigious NFL. One AFL team had a particular propensity to lose future stars to its rival league. In 1962, they picked Merlin Olsen, and he signed with the Rams and had a Hall of Fame career with them. Two years later, they drafted offensive tackle Bob "Boomer" Brown, who liked to display his strength by shattering four-by-fours with his forearm. Boomer opted to sign with the Eagles, and in his 10 years in the NFL, which also featured time with the Rams and Raiders, he was a frequent All-Pro. The following year, 1965, they picked Dick Butkus, but he signed with the Bears, and you know the rest. Ironically, this club traded the first-round pick in that '65 draft to the Jets, who selected Namath and then signed him. They continued to be snakebit. In 1967, the NFL and AFL agreed to hold a combined draft, and the following year this team picked Curley Culp, but they thought he might be too small to be an effective nose tackle, so they traded him to Kansas City before the start of the season. He went on to have an excellent 14-year career, primarily with the Chiefs and Oilers. Wow! Think about what a team they would have had with Namath at quarterback, Brown at offensive tackle, Culp and Olsen on the line, and Butkus at linebacker. It's no wonder that starting in 1963, they had 10 straight losing seasons and their winning percentage over the decade was less than .300. Name the team.

146. It was no secret that when Mike Ditka and Forrest Gregg, coach of the Bears' NFC Central rival Packers, were squaring off for a few years in the 1980s, they couldn't stand each other. Meanwhile, there was no love lost between the head guys from two AFC Central rivals, the Bengals and the Oilers. In a decisive game late in the 1988 season, Houston whipped Cincinnati, 41–6, and the Bengals' coach thought his adversary intentionally ran up the score. He was steamed, and even though the Bengals won the division and went on to the Super Bowl, the memory of his opponent's unsportsmanlike conduct festered. The following year, the Oilers nipped the Bengals in Houston mid-season, 26–24, and when they met in Cincinnati for a key game the next-to-last Sunday of the season, it was payback time. The Bengals crushed the Oilers, 61–7, and at his postgame press conference, their coach minced no words: he said he piled on the points to repay the Oilers' coach for what he had done the previous season. Revenge became complete when the Oilers, in position to win the division the last week of the season, lost to the Browns in the final minute and then dropped their first-round wild-card game to the Steelers in overtime. Soon after, the Oilers' coach and the team mutually agreed to part ways. He picked up the Falcons' vacant coaching position in the off-season and held the job for four years. He wasn't too broken up when the Bengals' coach got the ax after a 3–13 season in 1991. The Bengals' coach later coached the Buccaneers. Name these archenemies.

147. Every so often to make things interesting, Ditka would pull some razzle-dazzle out of the playbook by calling an option: Mac would hand off to Walter Payton and then go out for a pass; if he was open, Payton would try to hit him. They had some success with the play, as Wally connected with Mac for touchdown passes in '83 and '85 and a 42-yard completion in '84. But make no mistake about it—while Mac didn't mind running a pass route once in a while, he was no more interested in becoming a wide receiver than he was in joining the McCaskeys for a monthlong family vacation. There have been some players, though, who were versatile enough to see action at quarterback *and* wide receiver. In 1968, a rookie quarterback for the Broncos (who was just 5′11″, 180 pounds), operating out of the T-formation, threw 14 touchdown passes and was an excellent scrambler, averaging 7.5 yards on his 41 runs and punching the ball across three times. Although this man showed promise as an NFL signal caller, the Bills, who obtained him in a trade after the season, used him as a wide receiver, and he remained at that position the rest of his career. He was a good receiver, especially in 1970 when he led the AFC in catches and yards receiving for Buffalo. He later played for the Dolphins, Chargers, Lions, and Patriots. A quarterback active in 2002, renowned for his speed and moves, started a few games at wide receiver when he was younger. He caught 14 passes and a touchdown in 1995, his rookie season; made 17 catches, including 3 for pay dirt in '96; and caught 9 more in '99 and another TD. Mac expects you'll identify the current player in a snap, but he will be duly impressed if you pluck the name of the old-time quarterback/wide receiver.

148. Most players go straight from college ball to the NFL, but some guys, including star quarterbacks Kurt Warner and Jeff Garcia, take a detour and play in another league first. Match these players with the leagues in which they saw action prior to getting started in the NFL. And just so we can't be accused of trickery, we'll tell you that Doug Flutie's years with the CFL were *after* his first stint in the NFL (before which he played a season in another league), and while Darren Bennett played in the World League in 1995, he had been on the Chargers' practice squad the prior year; he played seven seasons in a different league before that.

A. Canadian Football League
   (Calgary Stampeders)   Kurt Warner

B. Arena Football League (Iowa
   Barnstormers)   George Koonce

C. United States Football League
   (New Jersey Generals)   Doug Flutie

D. Australian Rules Football League
   (West Coast and Melbourne)   Jeff Garcia

E. World League (Ohio Glory)   Darren Bennett

149. When Buddy Ryan, who had battled the Philadelphia media and owner Norman Braman for five years, was fired as Eagles coach following the 1990 season after his team was knocked out in the first round of the playoffs for the third straight year, many wondered if Buddy's ego would stand in the way of his getting another head coaching job. There were no bites for two years, but in 1993, the Oilers hired Buddy—not as head coach but as their defensive coordinator. He didn't do his reputation as a hothead much good when during a game in the '93 season, he got into an argument on the sidelines with Oilers offensive coordinator Kevin Gilbride and drilled him with a punch. But luckily for Buddy, Phoenix was on its way to its ninth straight losing season and offered him the head coaching job in '94 with the hope that he would bring some much-needed fire to the Cardinals. Upon accepting the position, Buddy declared with his usual modesty, "Y'all got a winner in town." He must have been talking about somebody else because his Birds went 12–20 over the next two seasons, and the ax fell on Ryan. Mac was part of the '94 squad, which at least posted a respectable 8–8 record, but he didn't have a high regard for Buddy's asinine approach to offense. The Cardinals were loaded with offensive weapons, but he just didn't get the most out of them. See if you can remember these four offensive starters on the 1994 Arizona Cardinals.

A. Buddy liked the running game, and this guy was the Cardinals' leading rusher that year with 780 yards, although he had gained more than 1,000 in '93, his rookie season. Arizona traded him to the Jets after the season—for a player with the same last name.

B. He was listed as a running back, but catching the ball has been his real skill. He caught 77 for Buddy's boys in '94, and 101 and 99 the next two seasons. He's the all-time receptions leader among running backs; he caught his 800th pass in 2002.

C. Originally a first-round pick by the Dolphins, this starting receiver for the Cardinals was pretty good, but not as good as he thought he was. He caught 38 for the Cardinals in '94 (without a touchdown) and 262 in his NFL career, 14 for touchdowns. Those numbers are not high enough for somebody who was so impressed with himself that he legally changed his middle name to "Thrill."

D. This wide receiver had 51 catches and five touchdowns for Arizona in 1994, and he was hauling in passes for another NFL team in 2002. Can you name him?

🏈 **150.** Mac spent much of his mild-mannered, well-behaved youth living in California, played some of his high school and all of his college ball in Utah, and currently lives in Illinois with wife, Nancy, and the kids. Can you name the state in which Mac was born? Stuck? Here's a hint: "The Wild Thing" also has ties to this state. His wife, Irene, is a native of Cinnaminson, a town in the south central part of the state, and her father, Rocky, is a longtime owner of a successful bowling alley in nearby Pennsauken called Maple Bowl Pub. Name the state.

A. New Jersey
B. Indiana
C. Texas
D. Pennsylvania
E. North Carolina

Deep Passes into Double Coverage

Who Am I?

🏈 151. I may not have been the best at spotting receivers downfield, but I certainly had the uncanny ability to spot boogers on my coach's shirt. During morning practice one training camp my rookie year as a Charger in 1989, I broke out laughing when I saw a mammoth booger on Coach Dan Henning's shirt. By the afternoon practice, three hours later, it was still there, which the ever-observant Jim McMahon did not fail to take notice of. Coach was giving Jim some crap about his flashy Zubaz pants, and he shot back, "At least I don't walk around with a booger on my shirt." Henning didn't hesitate to get his digs in, either. I was a little chunky around the middle, and he used to rib me, "You're the fattest young man I have ever seen in my life." I don't know if my weight had anything to do with it, but I struggled on the field my rookie year. Splitting time with

Mac and David Archer, I completed fewer than half of my 185 passes and threw only five touchdowns. I got a lot more playing time the following year after Jim departed to Philadelphia, and I tossed 16 touchdown strikes. That's the most I ever threw in one season during a career in which I was inconsistent, injury prone, and well traveled—I also played for the Falcons, Oilers, Chiefs, and Saints. Who am I?

● **152.** Jim had the opportunity to see me play at a combine designed to showcase players a few weeks before the 1982 draft. He wasn't particularly impressed with my ability: "This guy was the quarterback for Ohio State?! He sucks!" The Baltimore Colts' brass must not have thought so because they made me the fourth pick overall in the draft. (The Bears made Jim the fifth pick.) They soon regretted it. Mike Pagel beat me out for the Colts' starting quarterback job, and I didn't throw a single touchdown pass my rookie year. To make matters worse, I had somewhat of a gambling problem, which the league found out about, and they asked me to take a year off. (In other words, they suspended my sorry ass.) I was back to give it another shot in 1984, by which time Bob Irsay had relocated the Colts to Indianapolis. The change of scenery didn't help me—I threw three touchdowns in '84, none in '85, and my NFL career was over. I later played some Arena ball, and while quarterbacking for Detroit, I was named MVP of the Arena Bowl in 1990. Who am I?

153. Two years after the Bears made Mac the fifth overall pick in the 1982 draft, the Eagles chose me, a wide receiver out of Penn State, as the fourth pick in the '84 draft. I set quite a few PSU receiving records and was one of their big guns when they won the national championship in 1982, my junior season. I was glad the Eagles drafted me because I went to high school in South River, New Jersey, not far from Veterans Stadium. Drew Pearson and Joe Theismann played ball at South River High in the 1960s. A separated shoulder sidelined me for a few games my rookie year, but I got enough playing time to catch 26 passes, and I broke one for an 83-yard touchdown. The next three years, I averaged 30 catches—at 18 yards per shot—and three touchdowns. But then, even though I was healthy, playing well, and only 26 years old, I *retired*. Those rabid Eagles fans asked, "Why in the world is he doing that!" You see, I had what I thought was a sharp business mind—I majored in finance at Penn State and regularly read the *Wall Street Journal*—so I decided to open this restaurant in New Jersey; our specialty was chicken. The restaurant wasn't quite the smashing success I envisioned it would be, and a year later, I figured that I better resurrect my football career. I signed with the Oilers, but I saw limited action and caught only four passes in 1989. And then I headed back home to Philly where I was teammates with Jimmy Mac in '90 and '91. By that time, though, I had lost a step, and Calvin Williams and Fred Barnett were locked in as the starting receivers. I played infrequently, catching only five passes over the two seasons and returning six kickoffs. Good thing I got to see the amusing antics of Mac, Ron Heller, and David Archer and listen to Reggie White's entertaining impersonations of Hulk Hogan and Bill Cosby. Otherwise, I'd just as soon have stayed in the chicken business. Who am I?

🏈 154. I played for seven coaches in my 16-year NFL career, and I can say without doubt that none of them hated to lose as much as Michael Keller Ditka. Early in the 1983 season, my seventh and final year with the Bears, we lost tough, back-to-back games in overtime to New Orleans and Baltimore. When he returned to the locker room right after the Colts loss, Mike took out his frustration by punching a locker. He normally said a prayer when the whole team was back in the locker room, but this time he pointed to me and said, "You lead them in prayer. Doc, I need to see you." When Jim and the other players stopped laughing, I said the prayer, while Mike went and got his hand casted. Luckily, we won the following week; otherwise, he probably would have broken his other hand. I competed mainly with Mike Phipps, Bob Avellini, and Jim for quarterbacking time in Chicago and later played nine years with the Raiders, where I was primarily a backup to quarterbacks that included Jim's BYU teammate Marc Wilson, Jay Schroeder, and Steve Beuerlein. Who am I?

🏈 155. As long as NFL football is played, the rookies will be subjected to some good-natured ribbing and practical joking by the veterans, and I received more than my share during my first training camp with the Chargers in 1989. To give you a taste of it, one night a few of the vets tied me and another rookie up and dropped us in the parking lot at the college dorm where we were staying. At least they were kind enough to give us each a pillow so our heads weren't on the pavement. We got a little scared when we heard the revving of an engine nearby and looked over and saw a car heading toward us. We quickly rolled ourselves out of the way; otherwise, we would have had some nasty tire tracks all over our bodies. I caught a glimpse of the guy behind the wheel, and it was none other than that ball-busting Jim McMahon. I played in the backfield with Mac, and at 6′1″, 248 pounds I didn't have blazing speed, but I was packed with power. I led the Chargers in yards rushing my rookie season and each of the following four years, with a high of 1,225 in 1990. Unfortunately, when the Chargers made it to the Super Bowl following the 1994 season, I was gone—to New England, where at least I led the Pats in rushing and pounded into the end zone eight times. Our coach, Bill Parcells, and I had a disagreement late in the season, and he made the mistake of benching me in the play-off game, which we lost. I played one more season, with the Oilers as a part-timer, and that was it. Who am I?

◀▦▶ 156. It doesn't bode well for your career when you are drafted as a quarterback by a team that later that month acquires a quarterback in a trade who was picked in the same draft, who will go on to become one of the greatest of all time. That's what happened to me. After I had a strong career at Texas A&M, Denver chose me in the eighth round of the '83 draft. The problem for me was, at the same time, the Broncos traded for John Elway, who was disgruntled with the team that drafted him. I was John's backup for nine years, and while I learned a lot about quarterbacking from watching him, I didn't get much of a chance to play. I started only on the rare occasions when John was out with an injury; I averaged only 33 passes a season with a high of 75 and tossed 14 career touchdowns. After warming the bench for nine years, I retired as a player and turned to coaching. In that role, I have been quite successful. I collected a Super Bowl ring as quarterback coach for the 49ers in the 1994 season and two more rings as offensive coordinator for the Broncos in the 1997 and 1998 seasons. Who am I?

157. I was teammates with Mac the seven years he was with the Bears and had the pleasure of witnessing some of the classic exchanges between him and Mike Ditka. I remember this one time, Mac, as often was the case, didn't think much of the play that Ditka sent in and called an audible at the line, a running play to Walter "Wally" Payton. I was supposed to throw a block for Wally but somehow missed the audible, and he got nailed for a loss. On the sideline after the play, I could hear Ditka calling Jim a series of names not suitable to be repeated in front of a young audience. Although I missed that block, I delivered many for

Wally over the years and carried the ball a little myself. On the average, in the glory years of the mid-1980s, I would run the ball eight, nine times a game, and over the course of the season, I would score three or four touchdowns and also catch 35 to 45 passes. Who am I?

158. The Phoenix Cardinals picked me as a quarterback out of Ohio State in the third round of the 1988 draft. I had a hard time staying in the starting lineup for the Cardinals, because I was completing only about half my passes and worse yet was throwing more than twice as many interceptions as touchdowns. Phoenix finally ran out of patience after four years, and I sat on the bench for a year each in Indianapolis and Cleveland, wondering if I shouldn't be considering another line of work. But then I salvaged my football career by resurrecting my true talent—punting—and became one of the NFL's best booters over the next few years. I led the AFC one year in punting average, made the Pro Bowl another year, and played in the Super Bowl two other years. Who am I?

159. The 1984 season was a tough one for avid Steelers fans: two of their heroes from the Super Bowl years, Terry Bradshaw and Mel Blount, retired in the off-season; Franco Harris was cut in the middle of training camp; and Jack Lambert suffered a toe injury in the first game, which sidelined him for most of the season and led to his early retirement after the season. That year was my first with the black and gold; the Steelers drafted me in the first round out of Southern Mississippi, and I came through with a Rookie-of-the-Year performance, as I caught 45 passes—9 for touchdowns—and even ran a punt back for six points. My stats were even better in 1985: 59 receptions (for 1,134 yards), 12 touchdowns, plus 2 more on punt returns, and a trip to the Pro Bowl. I never duplicated my '85 year, but I had a few more good years with the Steelers, catching at least 50 passes four straight years in the late 1980s and early 1990s. Who am I?

160. While Jimmy Mac was the best Bears quarterback of the 1980s hands down, I arguably got the nod as the team's number one QB of the 1990s. Before I signed with the Bears in 1994, I had shown Jim's flare for winning. For the Lions in '91, I replaced Rodney Peete in the middle of the season and led them to six straight wins down the stretch and a trouncing of the Cowboys in the first round of the play-offs. In '93, Rodney and Andre Ware were doing most of the quarterbacking for Detroit the first 12 games; we were 7–5 and fighting for the NFC Central. I took over the job in Week 13 and led the Lions to wins in three of the last four games—tossing eight touchdowns along the way—and we nosed out the Packers and Vikings for the division. When I signed with Chicago in '94, Steve Walsh got most of the snaps, but I was the usual starter the next four years, except in '96, when a neck injury put me on injured reserve for most of the season. I threw 63 touchdowns my five years in Chicago, with a high of 29 in '95. That year, I also had three 300-yard games and set a Bears record by throwing 174 consecutive passes without an interception. The way my pro football career started, it's a wonder I ever turned into a starting NFL quarterback, let alone a good one. I wasn't drafted in 1987 when I came out of North Carolina State. The Saints signed me as a free agent, but they sent me packing at the end of camp. When the strike halted play two games into the regular season, the Falcons picked me up as a replacement player, and I saw action in three games. They cut me right before the '88 season, and I went north and signed with the Calgary Stampeders, where I had a woeful season, completing 40 percent of my passes and throwing 13 interceptions in only 153 passes. Who am I?

◖📧◗ 161. Mac and I were two of the quarterbacks on Buddy Ryan's 1994 Arizona Cardinals. I thought Buddy's offensive system put too much emphasis on the running game and not enough on the passing game and therefore wasn't conducive to scoring a lot of points. Mac sized up the offensive system more succinctly: it was dogshit. He couldn't understand why Buddy didn't take advantage more of the team's many great offensive weapons—and Jimmy didn't hesitate to let him know it. "Keep your opinions to yourself," bristled Buddy. "All we have to do is run the damn ball, and we'll win on defense." That year, the Cardinals did play a good defense—with ex-Eagle Seth Joyner and Aeneas Williams leading the way—as we allowed the fourth fewest points in the league. The problem was, Buddy's ultraconservative offense was ineffective, and we scored the second fewest points in the NFL and ended the season at 8–8. The next year, Mac and I were gone, and again Buddy's offense was lousy—the Cardinals scored the third fewest points in football—but his defense also stunk up the joint by allowing the most points in the NFL. Arizona stumbled to a 4–12 record, and after the season, Buddy found a pink slip in his mailbox. I had bounced around as a part-timer for a few years before I signed with the Cardinals and was a part-timer for a few years following my departure, but I finally found my groove after more than a decade in the NFL. For the Panthers in 1999, I tossed 36 touchdowns and led the NFL with 4,436 yards passing. I've got a good golf game, too, and I get to play with Mac every year in a tournament in Lake Tahoe—we usually make a friendly wager. Who am I?

162. In 1976, Joe Willie Namath's knees were just about shot, so the Jets drafted me in the first round, a quarterback who, like Joe, played his college ball for Bear Bryant at the University of Alabama. Future Notre Dame coach Lou Holtz had taken over the reins as the Jets' head coach at the beginning of the year, and it turned out to be a season to forget. Lou juggled Joe and me at quarterback, but we were both ineffective (we threw seven touchdowns and 28 interceptions between us), and the losses piled up. Holtz was so frustrated, he called it quits before the season was over—when the team was a dismal 3–10. The next year, Joe Willie was out in L.A. with the Rams, and Walt Michaels was in as the Jets' head coach. I showed some improvement over the next four years but still battled injuries, inconsistency, competition from other quarterbacks—such as the fleeting fan favorite Matt Robinson—and the boos from that critical Jets crowd. The boos were especially loud in 1980 when I threw 30 interceptions. I finally got it together in 1981, as I tossed 25 TDs and led the Jets to the play-offs for the first time since 1969. I hate to say it, but I was victimized by 4 interceptions by the Bills in the first-round play-off game (even though I threw only 13 during the regular season), and we lost, 31–27. The following year, I was sharp again during the season, which carried over into the first two rounds of the play-offs, as my passing helped us beat the Bengals and the Raiders. But then, the interception bug bit again—I was picked five times in the Jets' championship game loss to the Dolphins. I played one more year with the Jets, played two with the Saints, and then retired. On the whole, I may have taken my lumps during my career, but I rank third on the Jets' all-time list in yards and touchdown passes behind Namath and Ken O'Brien. Who am I?

163. With all the stars and characters on the 1985 Bears team, you didn't hear much about the kickers, but Mac will tell you that our place-kicker, Kevin "Butthead" Butler, and I, the punter, did a damn good job. I came over to the Bears toward the end of training camp in '85 by way of a trade with the Chargers, with whom I spent my first three years in the league. I had a good season in the Super Bowl year, averaging 42 yards per punt and landing 18 inside the 20-yard line. I was the Bears' punter in '85 and '86, and we won plenty of games those years, but when I reminisce about those two years with Bears teammates, I think we usually talk more about the temper of Mike Ditka than all the wins.

We used to refer to him as "Sybil" because it was almost like he had a split personality. He could be the most pleasant guy you'd ever meet, but he could turn around and get mad as a hornet even when we were doing well. One game in 1986, Mac rolled out and, instead of going short like Ditka called, went deep to Willie Gault and hit him for a touchdown. We're all congratulating Jim and Willie on the sidelines, but Ditka is fuming to me, "I didn't call that play! That little bastard is calling his own plays!" Yeah, but Mike, it was a touchdown for God's sake, not an interception. And I can't forget this tirade he went on in the locker room after a game in which we won but were a little sloppy. "You guys suck! I ought to cut all of you! You're all too ugly to be on TV! You couldn't get another job!" Mike didn't mind mixing it up with our defensive coordinator Buddy Ryan and was so angry once that he threatened to get rid of Ryan. Buddy wasn't too worried. "Screw you, Mike. You didn't hire me, and you can't fire me." I left the Bears after '86, was out of football for a year, played a season with the Giants, and then returned to Chicago for the last three years of my career. Ditka was still there, but Mac and some of the other hell-raisers weren't, so things were more subdued in my second stint. Who am I?

164. I hail from Wortham, Texas, a town 70 miles south of Dallas with a population listed at 1,020. It would be less than 1,000 if it weren't for my family—I have *21* half brothers and half sisters. You see, my father had 11 children from a prior marriage, while my mom had 10 kids from her previous marriage, before I was born. Things were always a little cramped at Thanksgiving. Maybe because I was the youngest and my parents fed me especially well, I stood 6′4″ and weighed 300 pounds—in *seventh grade*. It was about that time that I acquired an appropriate nickname, which has stuck: "Big." You won't be surprised that the other kids picked me first for teams in gym class. By the time I was in high school, I had really filled out—I was up to 6′6″, 370 pounds—but I was no fat load. I also lettered in track and basketball in high school, which shows you that I was quick and agile. Hitting people was my thing, though, and the University of Texas recruited me heavily at Wortham High. I started out for the Longhorns as a defensive tackle, but they switched me to the other side of the line sophomore year, and it was as an offensive tackle that I was picked second overall in the 2001 draft by the Arizona Cardinals behind Michael Vick. One of my half brothers, Charlie, played for the Steelers in 1974, where he was mentored by Joe Greene, who interestingly was the Cardinals' defensive line coach when I arrived in 2001. Charlie also played five years for the Cardinals—when they were still in St. Louis—after his season in Pittsburgh. Who am I?

165. On football's All-Time Wasted Talent, Bad Attitude team, I'm one of the starting running backs, along with that chronic malcontent Lawrence Phillips, who played a couple years with the Rams and Dolphins in the '90s. Tom Landry already had a strong backfield, with Calvin Hill (father of NBA star Grant Hill) and Walt Garrison (a rodeo cowboy in the off-season), when I arrived at the Cowboys' camp as a rookie in 1970. I dazzled Landry so much with my speed and moves that I got plenty of playing time, leading the 'Boys with 803 yards on the ground and the NFL with a 5.3 rushing average. I ran for 135 and 143 yards in our two NFC play-off wins, and while I was held to 35 yards in the Super Bowl, I scored Dallas's only touchdown on a passing play. In the off-season, I was bitching about how big a raise I deserved, which carried into the preseason and the start of the season; by the time it was resolved, I had missed three games. I was in the lineup the rest of the year, and though I had angered the Cowboys' brass and alienated my teammates, I hadn't lost my touch as a runner—I gained almost 800 yards in my 11 games and scored 13 touchdowns, 11 on the ground. I kept it going in the postseason, scoring a touchdown in our wins against Minnesota and San Francisco in the play-offs and against Miami in the Super Bowl. At that point, I had the potential to be one of the game's elite running backs for the years to come, and I pissed it away big time. After my sensational season in '71, I again got into a salary dispute with Cowboys management, which got so nasty, they told me to hit the pike and traded me to the Chargers, who had acquired some other complainers in the off-season, namely Tim Rossovich and Lionel Aldridge. That deal was a complete washout, as I never played a down for the Chargers and went on to the Redskins. By that time, I was a certifiable head case, and I was reduced to a reserve role—I played two years in Washington, gaining 442 yards and not showing the signs of brilliance that I displayed in Dallas. My NFL career was over at the age of 26—and I only had myself to blame. Who am I?

166. Mac and I were teammates together one year with the Chargers and two years with the Eagles, and yes sir, we did have a good time together. In San Diego, the baseball park was next to the football stadium, and when Mac and I had the chance, we would sneak over and get some batting practice in with the Padres. The fun continued in Philly. I remember this one game we had in Atlanta. During the pregame workout on the field, Jim and I were kind of hungry and spotted a pizza vendor, a young girl in the stands. We didn't have any cash on us, so Mac made a very reasonable offer: a football for a pizza, but the bimbo said no. Her manager saw what was going on, came over, and reamed out the girl for turning down our generous offer. Because he was such a good guy, we gave him two balls for a pizza, and Mac and I plopped down next to one of the goal posts and started chomping away. Later, Coach Rich Kotite spotted Jim with pizza hanging out of his mouth and barked, "What the hell are you doing?!" Come on Rich, as if there was something wrong with catching a snack before the game. Speaking of Atlanta, that's where my career began in 1984 when the Falcons drafted me out of Iowa State. I sat on the bench most of my rookie year, but I was the starter in '85 and '86. Eventually, I made my way to Washington for a year and then San Diego and Philly; after that, I played some ball in NFL Europe. Who am I?

167. I won't hear Jim McMahon voice any disagreement if I say that Mike Ditka was a royal pain in the ass to play for when his team was *winning*, which they usually were when Mac was there. Good Lord, I can tell you firsthand what a bastard he was when his team was losing. The Bears picked me out of Stanford in the first round of the 1988 draft primarily to use as a blocking back for Neil Anderson. We won the division my rookie year, but in '89—when Mac had left town for San Diego—Mike was mostly smiles as we opened the season 4–0, but our eardrums were stinging when we lost 10 of our final 12 games to finish 6–10. We bounced back by going to the play-offs in '90 and '91; both years, I was second on the Bears to Neil in rushing yards, and the first of those seasons I even led the team in receptions with 47. But it was déjà vu in '92, as we started the year 4–3, and then things fell apart and we lost eight of our last nine to finish 5–11, tied for last place. Ditka's tongue-lashings got pretty nasty, and at the end of that disastrous season, he was gone—and so was I, to New Orleans. I played two lackluster years for the Saints, and they released me, which was just as well. If I had hung around three years longer, Ditka would have been my coach again, and if you think I would have liked to endure 6–10, 6–10, and 3–13 seasons for motormouth Mike, you're nuts. Who am I?

168. Take a survey of football fans and ask them who the career sack leader is among linebackers, and I'd bet the farm that more people would guess Lawrence Taylor than me. L.T. was unquestionably faster than I was, and he may have been stronger, but I don't think he was as mean. I would have fit like a glove on Mac's Bears teams with guys like Steve McMichael and Dan Hampton, who thrived on punishing the other team. It wasn't to be, however, as the

Rams, coached by John Robinson, picked me in the '85 draft. It took me some time to work my way into the starting lineup and earn the respect of my teammates (I pissed off the pro-union veterans when I crossed the picket line during the 1987 strike), but when I did, I became quite a force. I tallied 16½ sacks in both 1988 and 1989, had two more double-digit sack seasons in L.A., and then headed to Pittsburgh. I played three years with the Steelers' "Blitzburgh" defense, and in my second season there, I led the NFL with 14 sacks. It was then back to the NFC, where again I was number one in the league in sacks for the Panthers in '96. When it was all said and done, and I had to find something to do with myself besides creaming quarterbacks, I played 15 years and ranked third on the all-time sacks list with 160. I never enjoyed a post–Super Bowl celebration, but I played in *six* conference championship games, including three straight for three different teams ('95 Steelers, '96 Panthers, and '97 49ers). Regrettably, of the six, my troops came out on the long end of the stick only once—the '95 Steelers—and we couldn't put away the Cowboys in the Super Bowl. Who am I?

169. I'm one-half of the answer to a difficult football trivia question: who is the last pair of running backs on the same team each to gain 1,000 or more yards rushing in the same season? I'll tell you the other half of the answer: Kevin Mack. For the Browns in 1985, Kevin ran for 1,104 yards and I just squeaked over the millennium mark with 1,002. In fact, it looked like I wasn't going to make it as time ran out in the last game of the season, and I had 994. But a defensive penalty prolonged the game for a play, and I took advantage of the reprieve by gaining eight yards and finishing at 1,002. The following season, we didn't gain 1,000 yards between us; with Curtis Dickey getting a lot of backfield time, Kevin gained 665 yards, while I ran for only 277. After two more so-so years with the Browns, I moved on to the Redskins and regained the old touch; I rushed for 1,219 yards in 1990, again topped 1,000 in '91 (earning invites to the always-exciting Pro Bowl both years), and fell two yards short with 998 in '92—no defensive penalty on the last play of the game that year. I also *threw* a touchdown pass each of those three years. Then it was back to Cleveland where I was a part-timer for two years, and I played two more for the Ravens when the franchise moved to Baltimore. When my playing days were over, I had rushed for 8,261 yards— among the top 25 of all time—and caught more than 500 passes, all with little fanfare. Who am I?

170. My NFL career began horribly, ended horribly, and wasn't very good in between. The 49ers drafted me in the first round (third overall pick) of the 1967 draft after I won the Heisman, as insurance for starting quarterback John Brodie, who was in his thirties by then. In my rookie year, I got some playing time in relief of Brodie and showed I wasn't ready to be an NFL starting quarterback—or a third-string QB for that matter—as I completed just 23 of 50 passes and was picked off *seven* times for an abominable interception percentage of 14.0. I also punted for the 49ers, and to show you how bad a year it was, I was the NFL's 13th-ranked punter out of the 16 punters in the league. The 49ers kept me around, and while I kept punting, I played quarterback infrequently—some years, almost not at all—the next four years. Brodie was at the helm most of the time, and he still had what it took, especially in 1970 when he had one of his best seasons. An injury to Brodie in '72 sidelined him, and I got the opportunity to show my stuff, and I played respectably, passing for almost 2,000 yards and throwing 18 touchdown passes. Brodie retired after the '73 season, and I was expected to be the starter, but I separated my shoulder in an exhibition game and missed virtually the entire year. I split time in '75 with Norm Snead, with neither of us doing a bang-up job. After the season, the 49ers acquired Jim Plunkett, hoping he would be the answer to their quarterback woes, and I was off to Tampa Bay to join the first-year expansion team Buccaneers. What a calamity that turned out to be. Coach John McKay handed me the starting job, and our team's hapless offense averaged just nine points per game, we were shut out five times, and we finished the season 0–14. The Bucs released me after the season, and that was all she wrote for my playing career. I went into college coaching after I retired—returning to my alma mater—and had a very successful run with that team. Who am I?

171. I starred on the "Cinderella" 1985 Patriots, who came within a victory of bringing New England its first Super Bowl title. The Pats had a history of underachieving, and we started out the season true to form, losing three of our first five games. We then got hot, winning nine of our last eleven to finish 11–5 and earn a wild-card berth. I was one of the team's top performers; in just my second year in the league, I pounded out more than 1,200 yards on the ground and scored five touchdowns. It was in the AFC play-offs that we really brought our game to the next level—we won three straight games *on the road*, and I cracked the 100-yard mark in two of them. In the championship game, we beat the Dolphins, breaking an 18-game losing streak in the Orange Bowl. Our magic ran out when we faced a jugger-naut, Mac's Bears, in the Super Bowl, and their tenacious defense held me, I'm embarrassed to say, to *one yard* rush-ing. Our whole team managed just seven yards on the ground. My career went downhill in a hurry after the Super Bowl season. In 1986, I ran for just 427 yards, and my aver-age per carry was a lousy 2.8. In '87 and '88, I was mostly warming the bench, as I had only four carries each year, and my career was over at the age of 27. My younger brother Chris played major league baseball for 10 years; in fact, he was traded in 1989 from the Phillies to the Padres in a deal that included Mitch Williams's sidekick, John Kruk. Who am I?

172. The list of quarterbacks who never threw for 4,000 yards in a season does not include Jim Kelly, Joe Mon-tana, or Troy Aikman. The list of quarterbacks who threw for 4,000 yards in a season includes Lynn Dickey, Scott Mitchell, and me. Go figure. After playing semiregularly and semicompetently my first two years for the Packers in 1987 and 1988, I won the starting job in '89 and played like past and future Green Bay quarterbacks Bart Starr and Brett Favre. I led the NFL in completions with 353 and yards with 4,318, and I was fourth in touchdown passes with 27. My passing exploits that year earned me the nickname of "the Magic Man." All those yards and touchdowns kind of put me on a pedestal, and I was grieving about money to the Pack's GM in the off-season. I held out, missing all of training camp in 1990, and when I finally signed about the time the season was getting under way, I was a little rusty. The football gods made sure I really got my due for squawking about money when I injured my shoulder in a midseason game and was placed on injured reserve for the year. In '91, I split time with Mac's old teammate Mike Tomczak, and then Favre came along, and I collected splinters on my ass sitting on the bench in '92. I was then off to the Colts for two years and the Lions for two years, but by then I had lost my magic. Who am I?

173. At Brigham Young University, which Jim and I attended together for a year, we had to sign a morals clause promising that we would abstain from all sorts of enjoyable things like chewing tobacco, consuming caffeine, and drinking alcohol. Jim, of course, had no time for such ridiculous rules. Sometimes he had to get creative, like he would wrap up a leaf in bubble gum. One time, I asked him what he was chewing, and he said, "Bubble gum." I kidded him, "Why is your juice brown?" Jim couldn't understand why BYU had rules against chewing when tobacco juice was used to treat contusions. About my NFL career, which wasn't nearly as long or as successful as Jim's, I played six years for the Oilers, mostly as a second-stringer behind first Dan Pastorini and then Ken Stabler. My last two years I got more playing time, as I shared the job with Archie Manning and Oliver Luck. We had a devil of a time winning games, though: we went 1–8 in the strike-shortened 1982 season and followed it up with an atrocious 2–14 campaign. During one stretch over the two years, we lost *17* straight games. Who am I?

🏈 **174.** I met Bill Clinton long before Monica, Linda Tripp, and Ken Starr did. Back in the early 1980s, I was president of my high school class in Marion, Arkansas, and won a trip to the state capitol. On my tour, I met the future prez, who was Arkansas's governor at the time. Bill looked at my massive body (6'5", about 300 pounds) and said, "Son, you're going to be a pro football player one day." His detractors may crack that that was more accurate than some of the statements he made while in the White House. An offensive lineman, I was drafted by the Cardinals back in 1986, their next-to-last year in St. Louis, and was still playing in the NFL in 2002, making me the last surviving St. Louis Cardinals draftee. Many guys are starters in their early NFL years but once they reach 30, have lost some of their strength and quickness and don't play as much. I was an exception to the rule. I started only 16 games in my twenties and missed two full seasons because of knee and elbow injuries. But I bounced back from the injuries and was stronger and quicker than ever in my thirties. From 1993 through 2002, I started all but three games for the NFC teams for whom I played. During my career, I blocked for four quarterbacks who played in the Super Bowl; I'm sorry to say that I was not blocking for them the years that they went to the big game. Who am I?

175. A generation ago, when the NFL's quarterback ranks included the likes of John Hadl and Roger Staubach, I was one of football's best—on the other side of the line of scrimmage, at strong safety. I had a flare for tackling and recovering fumbles, but my real forte was intercepting—and returning the ball a good distance after I made the pick. In 1968, I had an auspicious rookie year for an AFL team, as I piled up eight interceptions and returned them for 230 yards, including a 96-yard dash for a touchdown. Two years later, when the NFL and AFL merged, with my team getting placed in the AFC, I again snagged eight passes of opposing quarterbacks and ran them back for 191 yards; an 86-yard return helped the old average. In '71, quarterbacks had figured out that they should avoid throwing the ball in my zone, and I was held to two regular-season take-aways. But in the AFC Championship Game against the Colts, a Johnny Unitas pass was deflected by my teammate Curtis Johnson and ended up in my hands. I followed one open-field block after another, and 62 yards later I crossed the goal line for a TD. The script was similar the next year: I intercepted only three during the season, but in a first-round play-off win against the Browns, I had two pickoffs. I also played in my first of three consecutive Pro Bowls after the '72 season. I really earned my invitation in 1973, as I matched my career high with eight interceptions, two of which I ran back for scores. In a game against the Steelers, I tied an NFL record with four interceptions. As usual, I picked up an interception in the play-offs and did the same in '74. I retired in 1977 with 34 regular-season interceptions and a terrific return average of more than 23 yards. If you can't remember my ability as a safety, maybe you'll remember my bald head. Who am I?

Mixed Bag

176. There are other people in this world besides avid fans of the old Cleveland Browns who can't stand Art Modell, and Jimmy Mac is one of them. Before Jim signed with the Packers late in the 1995 season, he had a three-month association with the Browns, and to put it mildly, the experience left a bad taste in his mouth. The Browns' head coach was a guy who, in Jim's humble opinion, was downright awful. After going through training camp and expecting to make the team, Jim was given this unusual news by the coach: "You're released, but why don't you stay in Cleveland because eventually we'll probably activate you." Jim took the man's word for it and moved his wife and four kids to Cleveland. Finally, after he had been sitting around at home for six weeks, one of the Browns' quarterbacks got hurt; Jim got the call and suited up for two games. But get this—he wasn't paid. Jim discussed the matter with the team's general manager who had the audacity to say, "Maybe we'll pay you; maybe we won't." The GM's nonchalance and rudeness were not well received by Jimmy Mac. When Jim had finished grabbing him by the throat and throwing him against the wall, he called his longtime agent/lawyer Steve Zucker and exclaimed, "Get me outta here, or I'm gonna kill this idiot!" Jim got his wish and signed with his old rival, the Packers, the next week. Can you name the Browns' coach and general manager who, by virtue of making Jim's life miserable for a few weeks, are overwhelming selections on his All-Bozo team? By the way, Jim never was paid for those two games, thanks to that untruthful deadbeat (Jim used slightly stronger words than that) Art Modell.

177. Here is one for you old AFL fans. This upstart league was christened in 1960, and for six years it was its own eight-team league, separate and apart from the NFL, with its own championship game. Then, for the next four years, the AFL champion met the NFL winner in the Super Bowl. In 1970, the leagues merged, and two conferences, the NFC and AFC, were created. Try these four zingers about "the other league" from the 1960s.

A. George Blanda quarterbacked this team to the AFL title in 1960 and 1961, the league's first two years.

B. This head coach led the Dallas Texans to the AFL crown in 1962. After the season, though, the franchise moved to Kansas City and became the Chiefs. In the '69 season, the same man led the Chiefs to a Super Bowl victory.

C. What an impressive run by this team—they made it to the AFL Championship Game five of the league's first six years. Coached by Sid Gillman, who was later elected to the Hall of Fame, they won in 1963 but went down the other four years.

D. This Boston Patriots runner set the AFL record with 1,458 yards in 1966 and came back the next year to gain 1,216.

178. Some of the biggest characters and Jim's best friends during his years with the Bears were offensive linemen, who kept those mammoth defensive linemen and linebackers at bay while he was in the pocket trying to find Kenny Margerum, Dennis McKinnon, or one of his other receivers. Here are descriptions of four. Name them.

A. This center was a Bear for a long time. He started with Chicago the year before Jim and stayed three years longer. He loved to eat— whether it was his food or somebody else's. Once, in the middle of dinner during training camp, another player, Tom Andrews, cramped up so badly that he fell off his chair and was hunched up on the ground. The center seized the moment; he grabbed Andrews's plate, said, "You won't be needing this anymore," and dumped the food on his own plate. Good thing he moved so fast; when "the Refrigerator" saw what happened to Andrews, he hurried over with his plate.

B. How highly regarded was this tackle? The Bears picked him in the first round of the 1981 draft ahead of future Hall of Famer Mike Singletary. The guy was large—295 pounds with legs like tree trunks. And how he enjoyed razzing those rookies during training camp. He and some of the other vets would do stuff like make the first-year guys stand up at dinner and sing their college fight songs. (Jim avoided being subjected to such humiliation by missing dinner at the opportune times.) If a rookie was getting too cocky after practice, a few of the veterans would tie him to the goal post until he promised to tone down his ego.

C. This All-Pro guard, nicknamed "the Buddha," was in the twilight of his career when Jim arrived on the scene in Chicago in 1982. In a game against the Lions that year, Ditka sent in a certain play that Jim didn't care for, and Mac called an audible at the line, a running play to Payton, which drew a puzzled reaction from "the Buddha." "We're running over your big ass," barked Mac. "Block!" After Payton picked up a good gain, the guard joked to Jim in the huddle, "Youngsta, any more surprises for the old man today?!"

D. A roommate of Mac's, this bruiser, who played guard, was picked by the Bears in the sixth round out of the University of Michigan in 1982. Jim's apt description of him: "The guy was nuts." His hobbies included collecting guns and going on African safaris. In the locker room, he used to eat chicken wings; when he was finished, unlike most normal human beings who would deposit them in the trash can, this maniac instead put tape on the bones and shot them across the room, trying to nail his teammates.

179. With Frank Gifford and Al Michaels calling the action, flanked by a steady stream of entertaining and outspoken color men such as Alex Karras, Howard Cosell, Don Meredith, Dan Dierdorf, Dennis Miller, and John Madden, ABC's "Monday Night Football" has been a huge hit with pigskin fans around the country since it kicked off in 1970. Here are five quick questions about teams that have been featured on one of sports' most successful shows.

A. Among teams who have made at least 20 "Monday Night" appearances, this club has the best winning percentage (.652 through 2002) on the show, fueled by a 14-game winning streak from 1975 through 1981.

B. The final score of this wild tilt in 1983 was 48–47. Do you remember which teams knocked heads in this "Monday Night" shootout?

C. What defending Super Bowl champion posted an 0–3 record in one season before Frank Gifford and company (only a handful of teams have dropped three "Monday Night" games in one season), losing the games by an average of 15 points?

D. These guys have played almost all their games on Sundays. They went 14 straight years without a Monday game on their schedule and have played only a dozen or so times on Monday since they came into the league in the mid-1970s.

E. On the other hand, this team has been the most frequent participant, squaring off more than 60 times and playing at least once on Monday every season since the inception of the show in 1970, except 1989.

180. Most standout running backs coming out of college don't make it through the first round of the draft without some team snapping them up. But once in a while, a star runner remains untouched until the second round or later. Four of the following pairs of running backs were first-round picks; the fifth pair didn't hear their names called until after round one was history. Name them.

A. Robert Smith and Emmitt Smith
B. Edgerrin James and Warrick Dunn
C. Fred Taylor and Jerome Bettis
D. Ricky Watters and Curtis Martin
E. Eddie George and Marshall Faulk

181. Here are five good, but not spectacular, quarterbacks who retired in the 1980s. Can you identify the only one in the group that threw more than 200 touchdowns in his NFL career?

A. Craig Morton
B. Danny White
C. Jim Hart
D. Brian Sipe
E. Lynn Dickey

182. Now we're going to give you names of five very capable receivers who called it a career sometime in the '80s. We were thinking about asking you to pick out the only one with 500 catches, but Mac changed the play at the last minute—good thing Ditka wasn't around—and wants to know the only receiver among the five who did *not* have 500 receptions.

A. Pat Tilley
B. Wes Chandler
C. Harold Jackson
D. Harold Carmichael
E. Dwight Clark

183. These two guys were Mac's kind of players—they were hard-nosed and gritty and played their butts off every week. They were defensive backs—one was a cornerback, the other a safety—in the same secondary for the old St. Louis Cardinals in the 1960s. The cornerback was small—just 5′9″, 170 pounds—and he arrived in St. Louis as a 17th-round pick out of Nebraska in 1961. After seven years with the Cards, he played a decade with the Redskins. The trademark of the safety, who played his entire 13-year career in St. Louis, was his toughness. One time, he had casts on both of his hands, and the team doctor told him not to play (which, at least, was more sensible advice than the Bears' doctor used to give Mac). He ignored the doctor's orders and even intercepted, which was a common occurrence for him and his longtime teammate. Each finished his career with more than 50 picks to rank in the top 25 on the NFL's all-time list. Name this pair.

184. Having the worst record in the NFL can't be all that great a feeling for a team, but there is one consolation: they get the first pick in the draft after the season (unless they have traded it away or there is an expansion team coming into the league). Some teams have taken advantage of the opportunity by picking guys who have turned into franchise players, like Bruce Smith (Bills in '85), Troy Aikman (Cowboys in '89), and Peyton Manning (Colts in '98). Teams have later regretted other players they picked first, such as Ken Sims (Patriots in '82), Vinny Testaverde (Buccaneers in '87), and Ki-Jana Carter (Bengals in '95). Do you remember these players, whose names were called first in NFL drafts?

A. The Saints had a tough decision whom to pick first in the 1981 draft: a Heisman Trophy–winning running back from the University of South Carolina or an All-American linebacker out of the University of North Carolina. They went with the Heisman winner, and he had two 1,000-yard seasons in his four years in New Orleans and remains the Saints' all-time rushing leader. He also had a pair of 1,000-yard years for the Redskins. Still, they wonder to this day what if they had chosen the linebacker instead: Lawrence Taylor.

B. In the 1984 draft, New England first selected this wide receiver out of Nebraska, where he earned his degree in bible study. (That was Mac's second choice for a major.) He caught the Patriots' only touchdown in Super Bowl XX, which reduced the Bears' lead to 44–10. This guy's career stats were stellar: 851 receptions, 88 touchdowns, and 1,000-yard seasons for the Patriots, Dolphins, and Eagles.

C. The 1991 Indianapolis Colts were one bad team. Their record was 1–15, and they averaged a pathetic 9 points per game against 24 allowed. Naturally, they had the first pick in the draft the following year and grabbed a defensive tackle out of the University of Washington who had won the Outland Trophy in his senior year in college. A knee injury his rookie year with the Colts got his career off to a bad start, and he never completely recovered—he was finished by 1997. To make matters worse, by virtue of a trade, the Colts also had the second pick in the '92 draft, and they picked a Texas A&M linebacker. He, too, battled injuries, and by 1997, his career was also history. Name the tackle, and for extra credit, take a shot at the linebacker.

D. This man can stand next to Shaquille O'Neal and not look tiny—he's 6'7" and weighs 325 pounds. In 1997, he became the first offensive lineman in 29 years to be the number one pick in the draft. This horse has made it to the Pro Bowl and the Super Bowl, where he, Adam Timmerman, Tom Nutten, and the rest of the offensive line gave the quarterback plenty of protection, which allowed him to throw for a record 414 yards.

◀🏈▶ **185.** This diminutive kicker from Mexico got himself embroiled in some controversy, fueled by the egos of two opposing head coaches, late in the 1989 season. He started the year with Buddy Ryan's Eagles but had a cold streak and was waived halfway through the season. The Cowboys, whom he began his career with in 1987, picked him up to replace Roger Ruzek. About a month later, the Eagles went to Dallas on Thanksgiving Day and spanked the Cowboys,

27–0. During the game, an Eagle drilled the Cowboys' kicker, and afterward, frustrated Dallas coach Jimmy Johnson, in the middle of a disastrous 1–15 season, accused Ryan of putting a bounty on his kicker's head. Ryan flatly denied the charges, with typical Buddy flare: "Why would I want to knock out the other team's kicker who has been in a six-game slump?" Do you remember this kicker whose short career ended in 1989? Also, if you can, tell us the names of his two brothers—one who kicked for four teams over his 11-year career and the other who booted briefly for the Redskins and Packers.

186. You've heard and read a lot about Jim's record-setting college career at BYU, but his off-the-field adventures also make for amusing reading. For instance, he had this annoying habit of getting kicked out of houses in which he was living. Once during his sophomore year, he was living with a bunch of athletes, and they had this big party on a Saturday night. Some straitlaced students who lived nearby called security, and they got busted for underage drinking. The administration, which Jim admired so deeply, denied them the privilege of living in the house. Jim's antics over the summer when school wasn't in session were also entertaining. He wanted to earn some money his summer after junior year, and somebody offered him a job on a farm. His first assignment: clean out the barn. Jim's matter-of-fact question: "Which building is the barn?" When he was pointed in the right direction, he went to work; soon after, he was ordered to perform a rather unsavory chore: clean up the dead goat. Jim said *sayonara* and played golf all summer. We'll describe four guys who played ball at BYU and made it to the NFL, who undoubtedly had less tumultuous campus lives than Jim had. Name them.

A. This guy liked to fish about as much as Jim liked to golf. Jim thought he was the best defensive player on the BYU team during his years there. He played five seasons as a linebacker in the NFL, mostly with the Saints.

B. A quarterback, he won the Heisman Trophy for the Cougars in 1990. He was a backup in Green Bay to Brett Favre four seasons, seldom playing, and when he went down for the year with a thumb injury in November 1995, the Packers signed Mac, who was still seething over the way he was treated by the Browns. This Texan was also one of the quarterbacks on the new Browns in 1999, but not before he spent two years as the number one QB in Philadelphia and a year backing up BYU alumnus Steve Young for the 49ers in 1998.

C. In 1981, Mac's senior year, this bruiser was Jim's center. It was his freshman year at BYU, and he later snapped for Steve Young. He was also Young's center in the Niners' Super Bowl season in 1994, but he played most of his career for the powerful Giants teams of the mid-1980s to early 1990s. His brother went to

BYU before Mac's arrival and played tackle and guard for five NFL teams.

D. This Alaskan-born defensive tackle played at BYU, long after Mac, in the early 1990s. He was drafted by Atlanta in 1995 and took the leap from the Falcons' 3–13 debacle in 1996 to the Super Bowl in 1998.

187. Life doesn't get much better than kicking back on Thanksgiving Day, watching football, and gearing up for your mother's turkey dinner with your brothers, sisters, in-laws, and the rest of the family. As sure as mashed potatoes and stuffing will be on Mom's menu, the Detroit Lions will be on TV, doing battle on the gridiron. The Lions have played every Turkey Day since 1934 except for a six-year interruption during World War II. There is something about that day that must pump up the Lions because they usually play good ball, especially on offense—since 1983, they have scored 40 or more points on five Thanksgivings, and yet during that time, they have reached the 40-point mark three times in all of their other games combined. Try these questions about the Lions' long tradition of playing football on the fourth Thursday in November.

A. The Lions' Thanksgiving Day foe changes from year to year, but back in the days when Bobby Layne and Doak Walker were in the backfield and Joe Schmidt and Yale Lary were leading the defense, Detroit's opponent would

be the same each year. What team did the
Lions play every Thanksgiving from 1951
through 1963?

B. Mac thinks highly of this former Detroit head
coach, who was on the sidelines for nine
Thanksgivings, from 1988 through 1996. His
record was 5–4. He hasn't coached since his
Lions days, but he participates in Mac's annual
golf tournament, which of course is more
important. Who is he?

C. You shouldn't have to burn too many brain
cells trying to figure this one out. Four days
before Turkey Day 1992, on which the Lions
were edged by Houston, 24–21, who became
the Lions' all-time leading rusher? Take an
extra piece of pumpkin pie if you can
remember whose record he broke.

D. Do you remember the game in '97 when the
Lions, in Bobby Ross's first year as head coach,
rolled up 55 points, the most they have scored
in any game—Thanksgiving or otherwise—
since scoring 59 in the 1957 NFL Championship Game against the Browns. Which team
did Ross's Lions annihilate that day while you
were stuffing yourself?

188. Until Drew Bledsoe took a seat on the Patriots' bench in favor of Tom Brady in 2001, he had been New
England's number one quarterback, game in and game out,

since his rookie year of '93. Think hard—whom did Bledsoe replace as the Pats' number one quarterback in 1993? If you're drawing a blank, take a look at the five quarterbacks in the left-hand column and see if you recognize any as Drew's predecessor. While you're at it, try to match the four other quarterbacks, who were fixtures on one team for a long time, with the signal caller whose job they took.

A. David Woodley   Joe Namath (1965 New York Jets)

B. Dick Wood   Terry Bradshaw (1970 Pittsburgh Steelers)

C. Hugh Millen   Joe Montana (1980 San Francisco 49ers)

D. Dick Shiner   Dan Marino (1983 Miami Dolphins)

E. Steve DeBerg   Drew Bledsoe (1993 New England Patriots)

189. It was the hit that almost ended Jim McMahon's career. In Week 10 of the 1984 season, the Bears were hosting the Los Angeles Raiders at Solider Field. In the second quarter, Mac was in the pocket ready to throw a pass when the Raiders' nose tackle grabbed him by the shoulders and spun him around, and one of L.A.'s linebackers drilled him with his face mask. On the bench, Mac could hardly breathe and almost passed out. He was transported to the hospital by ambulance, and on the ride, Jim assessed the situation for the medical personnel: "It's my fucking kidney! Give me something for my pain!" When they finally made it to the hospital after getting stuck in a traffic jam on Lake

Shore Drive, tests showed that Mac had a lacerated kidney. The doctor told Jim he wanted to remove the kidney. Obviously, he wasn't aware of the NFL rule that provides that a player is not allowed to play with only one kidney because of the potential risk. Jim brought it to his attention in a hurry: "Bullshit! You're not cutting me!" The doctor did the smart thing and didn't cut him. Nevertheless, a lacerated kidney was no picnic—Jim had to spend three weeks in intensive care, where he lost 30 pounds. Worse yet, he wasn't allowed to drink for the entire three weeks. He was so thirsty for a beer after that, he would've had one even if he had to drink it with Randall Cunningham and Joe Theismann. The nose tackle that grabbed Jim played eight years for the Raiders—and was All-Pro in 1986—and followed that up with four years with the Jets. He had his best sack season in '84 with 12½. The linebacker who delivered the nearly career-ending hit spent his whole 11-year pro career with the Raiders after playing his college ball at Chabot Junior College in California. Jim would like to forget these guys. Can you remember them?

190. One of Mac's favorite pastimes when he was playing for the Bears was to bust the stones of kicker Kevin Butler. It was just good-natured ball-busting, though; Mac will be quick to tell you that "Butthead" made a big contribution to the Bears in the glory years, especially the Super Bowl season when he set an NFL rookie-season record for most points with 144. How good are you at remembering kickers for other teams in the 1980s? Let's find out. We're going to list 10 teams and ask you to name the place-kickers who saw the most action for them in the '80s. Seven out of ten right is really good; a perfect ten, and you'll get a pat on the back if Mac meets you. And for extra credit: which of these kickers didn't miss a game for his team (except three games in 1987 when replacement players were used) in the 1980s?

A. Atlanta Falcons

B. Detroit Lions

C. Los Angeles Rams

D. St. Louis/Phoenix Cardinals

E. Tampa Bay Buccaneers

F. Denver Broncos

G. Kansas City Chiefs

H. Miami Dolphins

I. San Diego Chargers

J. Seattle Seahawks

191. Mac may have had his differences with Mike Ditka and Buddy Ryan, and he may have thought Dan Henning and Dennis Green were not coaching geniuses, but he agrees they usually could hold a job for a few years, and if they got canned, they would get hired by another team. Leafing through the NFL's all-time roster of head coaches, we ran across some guys who had forgettable experiences running a team—they got the heave-ho after less than two years on the job, some after less than *one* year—and never returned to the head coaching ranks. Considering how they did, we can understand why they didn't make an owner's short list when he had a vacancy. These are some honest-to-goodness zingers, so you'll impress us if you can come up with even a couple.

A. Bills head coach Lou Saban quit after a 2–3 start in 1976, and the offensive line coach took over. He wished he hadn't. The Bills lost their last nine under him, and the losing streak reached 13 as they dropped their first four in '77 under Saban's replacement. Finally, he eked out a 3–0 win over the Falcons, but he won only two more the rest of the year. His final head coaching record: 3–20. Know his name?

B. Forty-niners owner Eddie DeBartolo celebrated many a Super Bowl victory in the 1980s and 1990s, but it was not smooth sailing from the beginning. When he bought the team in 1977, he brought in a new head coach to replace Monte Clark, and under him the Niners dropped the first five out of the chute. With Jim Plunkett at quarterback, they caught fire and won four in a row but then reverted to their early-season form by taking four of their last five on the chin, and they finished 5–9. The coach didn't get a second season to iron out the kinks with this team; he was dumped, and a new man was brought in. The new guy didn't make it even a year; a 1–8 start in 1978 found him looking for work, and he was replaced by the offensive coordinator, who after going 1–6 the rest of the way, didn't receive an invitation back. DeBart fired him and GM Joe Thomas. Any recollection of the three guys who coached the 49ers in 1977–78 before Bill Walsh took over?

C. Bud Grant had a long and impressive run as coach of the Vikings in which he led his troops to the Super Bowl four times. But after 17 years, he had had enough, and the Vikings promoted one of their assistant coaches to take Bud's place in 1984. It was a nightmare of a season, as Minnesota won only three games (and just by the skin of their teeth) against 13 losses. After the season, the Vikings brass quickly got on the horn with Bud, who said he was sick of hunting and fishing anyway, so he'd return as Minnesota's coach. Who replaced Bud during the 1984 season?

D. The good news for the Patriots in 1990 is they won one game. The bad news is the league scheduled 16. The Pats' rookie head coach that year had reason to be optimistic as his team lost a squeaker to the always-tough Dolphins on opening day and then beat the Colts the next week. Fourteen straight losses followed—and many of them weren't even close. They averaged 11 points per game while allowing 29. Guess what? The coach was given the inevitable news on "Black Monday" that his services were no longer required. Pats fans have tried hard to forget him; everybody else will have to try hard to remember him. Who is he?

192. Mac finished third in the 1981 Heisman Trophy vote behind a couple guys who had damn good pro careers—Marcus Allen and Herschel Walker. There have been some other Heisman winners over the years who went on to big things in the NFL, such as Paul Hornung, Tony Dorsett, Earl Campbell, and Tim Brown, but many others, to be blunt, didn't do shit. Put on your college football hats and belt out the names of these Heisman winners, whose college accolades far exceeded their NFL accomplishments.

A. Six years after Vinny Testaverde won the award in 1986, another strong-armed Italian quarterback from the University of Miami took home the trophy by beating out Marshall Faulk in '92. Marshall's NFL career has been slightly better than that of the guy who won the Heisman. He held the clipboard on the sideline for Mac's Vikings in 1993, appearing in one game. Three years later, he surfaced for the Seahawks where he appeared in his second and final NFL game; he threw one touchdown among his 16 passes.

B. Pretty fair season for this Florida State quarterback in 1993: he won the Heisman Trophy and led the Seminoles to the national championship, and then . . . *wasn't* drafted by an NFL team. Why? He was also a great hoops player and let it be known that he was leaning toward a career in pro basketball. So NFL teams passed on him, but the Knicks grabbed him, and he's been a steady but unspectacular NBA guard.

C. The Heisman jinx continued as the '94 recipient out of Colorado was picked in the first round by the Bears. He had a strong rookie year in Chicago, rushing for 1,074 yards and 10 touchdowns. Injuries began to hamper him the next season, and he gained 496 yards in '96, 112 in '97, and was done.

D. Only three wide receivers have won the coveted award since University of Chicago halfback Jay Berwanger won the first Heisman in 1935: Notre Dame's Tim Brown, who has been having himself a career that will take him to Canton; Michigan's Desmond Howard, who wasn't anything special as an NFL receiver, but was an outstanding kick returner; and a wide receiver out of Nebraska, who won the '72 award. No Hall of Fame career for him—he fell about 75 touchdowns and 600 catches short. After playing in the Canadian League for four years, he spent two years with the Chargers, who had originally drafted him in '73. His final NFL receiving stats: 17 catches, 246 yards, and 0 touchdowns. That's about two games' worth for Tim, although he would catch a couple TDs also.

193. As "The Wild Thing" told you in his baseball book, baseball Hall of Famer Dave Winfield was picked in the 17th round by the Minnesota Vikings in the 1973 NFL draft, even though he didn't play football at the University of Minnesota. Six years before, the Cowboys picked a man in the 11th round as a wide receiver, although he didn't run a single pass pattern at the University of Kentucky. He decided to pursue his number one sport—and made a good choice. Name him.

A. Fred Couples

B. Jimmy Connors

C. Tom Seaver

D. Phil Esposito

E. Pat Riley

🏈 **194.** Mac didn't care about personal awards—winning games and pulling practical jokes on his teammates were a much bigger deal to him—so he didn't give a rat's ass when he was named the NFL's Comeback Player of the Year in 1991. After not playing much his first year with the Eagles, he got his chance in '91 when Randall Cunningham went down with a season-ending knee injury in the first quarter of the opener. Mac battled some injuries himself that year, but he quarterbacked twelve games, and the Eagles won nine, including six straight down the stretch, which rallied the Birds into the thick of play-off contention. After that long-winded prelude, you may have guessed that this question is about Comeback Players of the Year. In the late 1980s, two L.A. Rams running backs were top comeback players in back-to-back years. One was drafted by the Browns in 1980, played part-time for them until 1984, and went to the Rams where he was a part-timer for two more years. Then in '87, when Eric Dickerson was traded to the Colts, he got his shot—and came through big: he led the league with 1,374 yards rushing and 11 touchdowns. The Dickerson trade also involved the Bills, and the Rams picked up a running back who had gained 1,100 yards as a rookie for Buffalo in 1984 and 883 yards in 1985. He didn't do much again until '88, when the Rams turned him loose and he ran for 1,212 yards and 16 touchdowns. As he was having his strong season, the first player again assumed a backup role and in fact didn't play anymore after that year. Our number two man came back with another big year in '89, but he was through by 1990, the year Mac watched from the Eagles sidelines, wondering how

Buddy expected to make the Super Bowl with Cunningham as his quarterback. Are these Rams runners ringing a bell?

195. If you were an American League baseball fan in the 1960s and 1970s, didn't you get sick of National League fans telling you how much better their league was because they kept winning the All-Star Game every year? They won 19 out of 20 games from the early '60s until the early '80s. Who knows whether it proved the National League was stacked with more stars? Don't worry—we're not going to quiz you on the Pro Bowl (if you care, the NFC and AFC are about even in the series, which began with the 1970 merger; the NFC won 8 out of 10 from the mid-1970s to the mid-1980s, which is the hottest streak either conference has put together) but on a streak in which the team from one of the two conferences won the Super Bowl several years in a row. To wrest the ball away from the cornerback and safety, pick out the conference—and the length of the streak. To break away from the defenders and outrun them to the goal line, tell us the years that the streak spanned and the team from the other conference that snapped the streak.

A. NFC—5 years
B. AFC—7 years
C. NFC—9 years
D. AFC—11 years
E. NFC—13 years

196. Mac will tell you that life as an NFL quarterback is copacetic when you're starting, healthy, and in the groove, but it can be quite a drag when you're carrying the clipboard, camped out in the trainer's room, or throwing the ball like crap. Guys like Dan Marino and John Elway, who were number one on the depth chart for a lot of years running, hardly ever got hurt, and usually stayed on their game, are a rarity. But for every Marino and Elway, there are a couple dozen men whose run as starting quarterback is short-lived. Injuries, inconsistency, great competition, or all of the above inevitably sent them to the sidelines. We'll throw you the names of 10 former quarterbacks who fit in that category, along with the years in which their arms got the best workout—when they set their career highs for passes in a season. Tell us what teams' uniforms they were wearing the years in question.

Team	Quarterback	Year	Passes
A.	Randy Johnson (not "the Big Unit")	1966	295
B.	Pete Liske	1971	269
C.	Marty Dombres	1972	222
D.	James Harris	1975	285
E.	Cliff Stoudt	1983	381
F.	Steve Pelleur	1988	435
G.	Bob Gagliano	1989	232
H.	John Friesz	1991	487
I.	Heath Shuler	1994	265
J.	Steve Bono	1995	520

◀💬▶ **197.** When the Bears stuck it to the Pats in Super Bowl XX, Mac threw 20 passes, which is fewer than most QBs toss in the big event; the average is about 25. It's hard to believe, but there was a Super Bowl in which the quarterback of the winning team threw just *seven* passes. He handed off 53 times—or almost 90 percent of the plays from scrimmage. It was the same script in the championship game they won: six passes and 53 runs. It's not as if the quarterback was some rag-arm like Gary Huff or Rick Mirer; this guy could throw the ball. After all, he was inducted into the Hall of Fame. Name the man who passed so sparingly in the championship game and Super Bowl, as well as the season.

◀💬▶ **198.** We were going to ask you the difference between a "franchise player" and a "transition player," an "unrestricted free agent" and an "exclusive rights free agent," and the "physically-unable-to-perform list" and the "injured-reserved list," but that would require some lengthy explanations, which Mac doesn't feel like providing because this is one of the last questions in the book, and he's tired. So we picked an easier term out of the football glossary to ask you questions about: "holdout." We're not going to ask you the definition because you'll know it refers to a player who gets in a contract dispute with his team and doesn't report until it's resolved. Contract squabbles are not uncommon—we've referred to a few in here—so we'll focus on the hard-core holdouts: guys who sat out an entire season because they were embroiled in a contract battle. Name them.

A. Two of Jim's teammates on the Bears held out a whole season, but they picked the wrong year to do it: 1985. One was a safety, the other a linebacker/defensive end. Both returned to the Bears in '86 but later signed with the Eagles and played for Buddy Ryan.

B. Who was the best quarterback in Saints history? It sure wasn't Dave Wilson. Our vote goes to this guy, a true Cajun who was born and attended high school and college in Louisiana. He led the Saints to their first three winning seasons (after 20 straight nonwinning years), from 1987 through 1989, but he was insulted by the Saints' contract offer, wouldn't give in, and sat out the '90 season. New Orleans played .500 ball the year of his holdout, and then he returned and directed them to two more winning seasons. He finished with four years in Atlanta.

C. The L.A. Rams corralled this gigantic defensive tackle in the first round (third overall pick) of the '92 draft. His 10½ sacks in his second year earned him a round-trip ticket to Hawaii after the season, but his production fell off, and after the '97 season he was traded to the Redskins. The winter after his first season in Washington, he got into a bitter salary dispute with the 'Skins management and didn't put the uniform on all year. In the off-season, the Panthers tendered an offer that Washington declined to match, so he flew south to Carolina.

D. It's a similar story for this defensive tackle who played college ball at Toledo. After four lackluster years with the Broncos, he was released in '96 and signed with another AFC team. He chalked up 10½ sacks that year, thought he had joined the NFL's elite pass rushers, and because his salary demand and the team's offer were so far off, he sat out the season to prove his point. He came to terms the following winter and went out and had half as many sacks as he did the season prior to the holdout.

🏈 **199.** When Mac recalls his days with the Bears and the guys he played with, he doesn't think only about the Super Bowl season and all of his nutty teammates that year. How could he forget his glorious rookie year of 1982 when he and Mike Ditka first became acquainted. Mac played with many guys who endured the 3–6 strike season in '82 and some losing seasons that preceded it but weren't around for the unforgettable ride in '85. Here are eight of those players: they all started their careers with the Bears in the 1970s—two as early as 1972 when Abe Gibron was head coach—and played long enough to hang out with Jimmy M. and Mike D., but not long enough to take home the ring. See if you can match them with their positions.

A.	Wide receiver (occasionally played defensive back)	Bob Parsons
B.	Free safety	Jerry Muckensturm
C.	Punter (saw some action as tight end)	Brian Baschnagel
D.	Defensive tackle	Robin Earl
E.	Running back	Willie McClendon
F.	Linebacker	Doug Plank
G.	Tight end (broke in as fullback)	Jim Osborne
H.	Offensive tackle/guard	Dan Jiggets

⬤▶ 200. Brown's occasionally raucous, football-loving cousin Leslie gets a big assist in the writing of this book for participating in the daylong interview of Mac at his home in Northbrook, Illinois. She jotted down notes as Mac regaled us with tale after entertaining tale. She caught a few things that Brown didn't. For example, Mac was talking about his junior high days, and Brown thought Mac said that he would throw firecrackers into an empty classroom. Leslie clarified that he threw them into a *full* classroom. In light of Leslie's invaluable assistance, it would be rather rude if a question were not dedicated to her. What would be more fitting than to have you name teammates of Mac's named Leslie?

A. For this man, Super Bowl XX was bitter-sweet—he picked up a Super Bowl ring as the Bears beat the Patriots, but it was the last game of his career at age 26. While making a tackle on a reverse, he sustained a serious knee injury, which prevented him from playing again. He and Mike Richardson were starting cornerbacks on those '85 Bears.

B. In Mac's year with the Chargers, the defense was loaded with excellent players such as Lee Williams and Gill Byrd, but the best was this defensive end who sometimes lined up at linebacker. He was usually good for about a dozen sacks a season (he had 12½ in 1989 when Mac was in town), and he piled up 132½ in his career, which puts him in the top 10. If it weren't for a knee injury, which shelved him for a year and a half early in his career, he might have been in the top five.

C. He went by Les, but his given name was Leslie. He was a reserve defensive lineman (6'7″, 290 pounds) who had two stints with the Chargers and also played for the Panthers and Saints. He got his name etched in the record books in 1990 for San Diego when he recovered two opponents' fumbles for touchdowns; he also had a TD on a fumble recovery for the Chargers in 1987, his rookie season.

Answers

Screen Passes Wide Open

1. Walter Payton
2. Dan Marino
3. Randall Cunningham
4. Earl Campbell
5. Herschel Walker
6. Marcus Allen
7. Steve Young
8. Junior Seau
9. Terrell Davis
10. Dick Butkus
11. Eddie George
12. Reggie White
13. Darrell Green
14. Jimmy Smith
15. Matt Millen
16. Joe Namath
17. Cris Carter
18. Jim Kelly

19. George Allen

20. Ahmad Rashad, previously known as Bobby Moore

21. Tiki Barber

22. Keith Jackson

23. Raymond Berry

24. Vinny Testaverde

25. Andre Rison

26. Green Bay Packers—Super Bowls I–II

    Miami Dolphins—Super Bowls VII–VIII

    Pittsburgh Steelers—Super Bowls IX–X

    Pittsburgh Steelers—Super Bowls XIII–XIV

    San Francisco 49ers—Super Bowls XXIII–XXIV

    Dallas Cowboys—Super Bowls XXVII–XXVIII

    Denver Broncos—Super Bowls XXXII–XXXIII

    A. Norton played on the Cowboys, who won Super Bowls XXVII and XXVIII, as well as the 49ers who won Super Bowl XXIX.

27. A. Clarke Hinkle

    B. Sammy Baugh

    C. Chuck Bednarik

    D. Bill George

    E. John Mackey

    F. Lem Barney

    G. Alan Page

    H. John Hannah

    I. Mike Webster

    J. Howie Long

28. Marv Levy

29. D. Bernie Kosar never won a Super Bowl. Hostetler—Giants, Super Bowl XXV; Rypien—Redskins, Super Bowl XXVI;

Plunkett—Raiders, Super Bowls XV and XVIII; and
Williams—Redskins, Super Bowl XXII

30. Atlanta Falcons

31. A. Chuck Howley
    B. Jake Scott
    C. Harvey Martin and Randy White
    D. Richard Dent
    E. Larry Brown
    F. Ray Lewis
    G. Dexter Jackson

32. A. Favre (through 2002)
    B. Aikman
    C. Moon
    D. Testaverde (through 2002)
    E. George

33. A. Eric Metcalf
    B. Desmond Howard
    C. Brian Mitchell
    D. Mel Gray

34. A. Hornung
    B. Jackson
    C. Swann
    D. Brown
    E. Nitschke

35. Starr—15 (Green Bay Packers)
    Namath—12 (New York Jets)
    Tarkenton—10 (Minnesota Vikings)
    Layne—22 (Detroit Lions)
    Marino—13 (Miami Dolphins)
    Montana—16 (San Francisco 49ers)

Elway—7 (Denver Broncos)

Simms—11 (New York Giants)

Unitas—19 (Baltimore/Indianapolis Colts, although he never played for them in Indianapolis)

Fouts—14 (San Diego Chargers)

36. B. Brian Bosworth

37. A. Red Grange

    B. Marion Campbell

    C. Jim Kiick

    D. Ken Stabler

    E. Ozzie Newsome

38. Joe Greene, Jack Ham, Terry Bradshaw, Mel Blount, Franco Harris, and Jack Lambert; Harris finished his career with the Seahawks.

39. Don Shula—Baltimore Colts (Super Bowl III) and Miami Dolphins (Super Bowls VI, VII, VIII, XVII, and XIX)

    Dan Reeves—Denver Broncos (Super Bowls XXI, XXII, and XXIV) and Atlanta Falcons (Super Bowl XXXIII)

    Bill Parcells—New York Giants (Super Bowls XXI and XXV) and New England Patriots (Super Bowl XXXI)

    Dick Vermeil—Philadelphia Eagles (Super Bowl XV) and St. Louis Rams (Super Bowl XXXIV)

40. A. Jaworski (Eagles)

    B. Esiason (Bengals)

    C. Krieg (Seahawks)

    D. Montana (49ers)

    E. Simms (Giants)

41. A. James Brown

    B. Marvin Harrison

    C. Roderick Coleman

    D. Rich Gannon

    E. Troy Vincent

42. Joe Gibbs. As coach of the Redskins from 1981 through 1992, he won the Super Bowl following the 1982, 1987, and 1991 seasons.

43. Herschel Walker (teammates on 1992 Eagles)—1,514 yards for 1988 Cowboys

    Roger Craig (teammates on 1993 Vikings)—1,502 yards for 1988 49ers

    Robert Smith (teammates on 1993 Vikings)—1,521 yards for 2000 Vikings

    Garrison Hearst (teammates on 1994 Cardinals)—1,570 yards for 1998 49ers

44. Morton Andersen (the lefty) and Gary Anderson (the righty)

45. Terry Glenn (New England Patriots), Joey Galloway (Seattle Seahawks), and Chris Sanders (Houston Oilers)

46. A. Steve Walsh

    B. Danny White

    C. Roger Staubach

    D. Don Meredith

    E. Jason Garrett

47. A. Frank Youell Field

    B. Franklin Field

    C. War Memorial Stadium

    D. Forbes Field

    E. The Polo Grounds

48. A. Ron Cox

    B. Herschel Walker

    C. O. J. Simpson

    D. Marshall Faulk

49. A. Fred Biletnikoff

    B. Lydell Mitchell

    C. Kellen Winslow

    D. Dwight Clark

    E. Al Toon

    F. Haywood Jeffires

    G. Sterling Sharpe

    H. Carl Pickens

    I. Muhsin Muhammad

50. A. Alan Page

    B. Chris Bahr

    C. Jeff and Jack Kemp

    D. Jason Sehorn

Down-and-Outs to the Sideline

51. William "the Refrigerator" Perry

52. Don Hutson

53. Jim Harbaugh

54. Joe Theismann

55. Eric Allen

56. Clyde Simmons

57. Bubby Brister

58. Ted Hendricks

59. Anthony Carter

60. Ed "Too Tall" Jones

61. Randall McDaniel

62. Tony Siragusa

63. Charles Haley

64. Tony Gonzalez

65. Dan Hampton

66. Nick Lowery

67. Chris Chandler

68. Rodney Peete

69. Leon Lett

70. Forrest Gregg

71. John Randle

72. Johnnie Morton

73. Bruce Matthews

74. Chris Weinke

75. Dorsey Levens

76. A. Jim Brown

    B. John Riggins

    C. Eric Dickerson

    D. Gerald Riggs

    E. Barry Foster

    F. Rodney Hampton

77. A. Bob Hayes

    B. Charlie Joiner

    C. Steve Watson

    D. Bill Brooks

    E. Gary Clark

    F. Brett Perriman

78. A. Marv Hubbard

    B. Ben Davidson

    C. George "Butch" Atkinson

    D. Otis Sistrunk

79. D. Tom Landry (Dallas Cowboys, 1966–85)

80. Seattle Seahawks

81. A. Dallas Cowboys (The Steelers beat them, 35–31, in Super Bowl XIII.)

    B. Miami Dolphins (They beat the Redskins, 14–7, in Super Bowl VII.)

    C. Minnesota Vikings (They have scored 7, 7, 6, and 14 points in their four Super Bowls, losing each time.)

    D. San Francisco 49ers (In Super Bowl XXIII, Joe Montana hit John Taylor for a touchdown in a 20–16 win over the Bengals.)

    E. Denver Broncos (In Super Bowl XXI, the Broncos led 10–9 at the half, but the Giants pummeled them in the second half by scoring 30 points, to win the game 39–20.)

82. A. Steve Young (Super Bowl XXIX)

    B. John Elway (Super Bowl XXXIII)

    C. Jim McMahon (Super Bowl XX)

    D. Joe Montana (Super Bowls XVI, XIX, and XXIV)

    E. Doug Williams (Super Bowl XXII)

83. A. Bears (1933, 1940, 1941, 1943, 1946, 1963)

    B. Lions (1935, 1952, 1953, 1957)

    C. Eagles (1948, 1949, 1960)

    D. Redskins (1937, 1942)

    E. Steelers

84. Green Bay Packers (1994–98). Their home records those years were 8–1, 8–1, 10–0, 9–0, and 7–1, and they were quarterbacked, of course, by Brett Favre, who gets especially hot when the weather is cold.

85. Gillman—49ers. He coached the Los Angeles Rams (1955–59), Los Angeles/San Diego Chargers (1960–69, '71), and Houston Oilers (1973–74).

Gregg—Chiefs. He coached the Cleveland Browns (1975–77), Cincinnati Bengals (1980–83), and Green Bay Packers (1984–87).

Knox—Vikings. He coached the Los Angeles Rams (1973–77, 1992–94), Buffalo Bills (1978–82), and Seattle Seahawks (1983–91).

Parcells—Raiders. He coached the New York Giants (1983–90), New England Patriots (1993–96), and New York Jets (1997–99).

Pardee—Cardinals. He coached the Chicago Bears (1975–77), Washington Redskins (1978–80), and Houston Oilers (1990–94).

Their regular-season winning percentages were: Parcells (.579 entering the 2003 season), Knox (.558), Gillman (.550), Pardee (.530), and Gregg (.469). Jim is really disappointed that Gregg finished last.

86. 1. Notre Dame (Dave Duerson)
  2. USC (Keyshawn Johnson)
  3. Ohio State (Pepper Johnson)
  4. Pittsburgh (Dan Marino)
  5. Purdue (Dave Butz)
  6. Florida (Emmitt Smith)
  7. Oregon (Norm Van Brocklin)
  8. Brigham Young (Todd Christensen)
  9. Wake Forest (Brian Piccolo)
  10. Yale (Dick Jauron)

87. D. Lorenzo Freeman

88. Jimmy Johnson. Johnson replaced Tom Landry when he was fired by Cowboys owner Jerry Jones after the 1988 season and Don Shula when he retired as Dolphins coach after the 1995 season.

Shula ranks first among coaches with 328 regular-season wins; Landry is third with 250. George "Papa Bear" Halas is second with 318 victories, which he accumulated for the Bears.

89. C. Dan Marino

90. A. Andre Reed
    B. Gary Larsen
    C. Lyle Alzado
    D. Jon Kitna

91. A. Jim Breech
    B. Cris Collinsworth
    C. Anthony Munoz
    D. Max Montoya
    E. Reggie Williams
    F. Turk Schonert

92. A. Andy Reid
    B. Jeff Fisher
    C. Mike Holmgren
    D. Marty Mornhinweg

93. A. The Jets' defensive line of the early 1980s, led by Mark Gastineau and featuring Marty Lyons and Joe Klecko.
    B. The Bills' offensive line of the early 1970s, who blocked for O. J. Simpson and therefore turned on "the Juice." Guards Reggie McKenzie and Joe DeLamielleure were the standouts.
    C. The massive offensive line for the Redskins that cleared the way for John Riggins in the early 1980s; they included George Starke, Jeff Bostic, and Joe Jacoby.
    D. The receivers from the same Redskins team, including Alvin Garrett, Charlie Brown, and Art Monk, who liked to

celebrate after scoring a touchdown by getting in a circle and high-fiving each other.

E. The Dolphins' defense for Don Shula's excellent teams of the early 1970s. They lacked superstars but abounded with steady performers such as Bob Matheson, Doug Swift, and Tim Foley.

F. The Steelers' impenetrable defense from the Super Bowl years of the mid- to late 1970s. It was usually used to describe their defensive line, which featured "Mean" Joe Greene and Dwight White.

G. The Rams' defensive line in the mid-1960s. It consisted of Deacon Jones, Merlin Olsen, Rosey Grier, and Lamar Lundy.

H. The Broncos' nasty defense from the late 1970s. Coach Red Miller's unit included Randy Gradishar and Lyle Alzado.

I. The Cowboys' defense from the early 1970s; key cogs on their D included Bob Lilly and Lee Roy Jordan.

J. The Dolphins' defense of the mid-1980s. By coincidence, the last names of several of their defensive starters began with the letter B; Bob Baumhower, Kim Bokamper, and Lyle Blackwood were among them.

94. A. Steve Largent
    B. Lance Alworth
    C. Frank Gifford
    D. Pete Johnson
    E. Harold Carmichael
    F. Charley Taylor
    G. Dalton Hilliard
    H. Lenny Moore

95. E. Paul Krause intercepted 81 passes during his career with the Redskins and Vikings from 1964 through 1979. Lane recorded 68 picks, Lott 63, Thomas 58, and Walls 57.

96. A. 6. The Raiders picked Charles in the first round of the '98 draft; the Steelers nailed Rod in the first round of the '87 draft; the Cowboys went for Darren in the second round of the '92 draft.

    B. 4. Rod played for San Francisco in 1997; Charles and Darren haven't played for the 49ers.

    C. 2. Darren was a linebacker at Arizona State, and the Cowboys switched him to safety.

    D. 1. Charles won the award for the University of Michigan in 1997.

    E. 7. Through 2002, Charles and Darren have played in 4, and Rod in 11.

    F. 5. Darren has rings from the Cowboys' championship teams from 1992, 1993, and 1995; Rod picked up one when the 2000 Ravens won the Super Bowl.

    G. 3. Rod has 69 through 2002.

    H. 8. Rod played at Purdue, and as we mentioned, Darren played at Arizona State and Charles at Michigan.

97. B. The Jags' 14–2 record in 1999 was the best in the NFL. They decimated Miami, 62–7, in the divisional play-offs but ran out of steam in the AFC Championship Game and lost to Tennessee, 33–14.

98. Jack (end) and Jim (linebacker) Youngblood

99. Jim Mora

100. A. Chiefs (35–10 in Super Bowl I)

    B. Bills (52–17 in Super Bowl XXVII)

    C. Ravens (34–7 in Super Bowl XXXV)

    D. Raiders (38–9 in Super Bowl XVIII)

    E. Chargers (49–26 in Super Bowl XXIX)

Slants Across the Middle

101. Doug Flutie
102. Andre Waters
103. Jason Elam
104. Willie Gault
105. Michael Dean Perry (brother of "the Refrigerator")
106. Trent Dilfer
107. Mickey Shuler
108. Dan Wilkinson
109. Gary Fencik
110. Roy Green
111. Kerry Collins
112. Qadry Ismail (brother of Raghib "Rocket" Ismail)
113. Ken Anderson
114. Elvis Grbac
115. Anthony Miller
116. Mo Lewis
117. Marc Wilson
118. Tony Boselli
119. Archie Griffin
120. Yancey Thigpen
121. Robert Porcher
122. Sonny Jurgensen
123. Rulon Jones

124. Darren Bennett

125. Derrick Alexander

126. A. False. It didn't take him that long—he got sent to the principal's office his *first day* of kindergarten for picking on another kid.

   B. False. Jim hated to study and, as a result, report card day wasn't his favorite.

   C. False. When Jim had a chance to trade punches with a classmate, be assured he took advantage of it.

   D. False. Jim was known to talk back to teachers and even spat on a couple of the most intolerable ones.

   E. False. He was smoking two packs of cigarettes a day when he was 12.

   F. False. Baseball was his game when he was young, although getting kicked off the junior high team by the coach (who happened to be his father) for smoking cigarettes dampened his enthusiasm.

   G. True. When he finally got caught, he had to clean it up, which took two weeks.

   H. False. Jim racked up *16* pink slips in high school.

   I. False. Actually, his father threatened Jim that if he didn't shape up, he'd end up in a boys' home or prison.

   J. False. Jim's usual response was, "Shut the fuck up. I'm trying to get some sleep."

   (*Editor's note:* Looking back on his childhood, Jim realizes he was a hellion and discourages kids from behaving like he did.)

127. A. Young

   B. Elway

   C. Favre

    D. Everett

    E. Brunell

128. George Blanda (26 years)—Chicago Bears, 1949, 1950–58; Baltimore Colts, 1950; Houston Oilers, 1960–66; Oakland Raiders, 1967–75

    Morton Andersen (21 years)—New Orleans Saints, 1982–94; Atlanta Falcons, 1995–2000; New York Giants, 2001; Kansas City Chiefs, 2002

    Gary Anderson (21 years)—Pittsburgh Steelers, 1982–94; Philadelphia Eagles, 1995–96; San Francisco 49ers, 1997; Minnesota Vikings, 1998–2002

    Earl Morrall (21 years)—San Francisco 49ers, 1956; Pittsburgh Steelers, 1957–58; Detroit Lions, 1958–64; New York Giants, 1965–67; Baltimore Colts, 1968–71; Miami Dolphins, 1972–76

    Darrell Green (20 years)—Washington Redskins, 1983–2002

    Jim Marshall (20 years)—Cleveland Browns, 1960; Minnesota Vikings, 1961–79

    Jackie Slater (20 years)—Los Angeles Rams, 1976–94; St. Louis Rams, 1995

129. A. Jan Stenerud

    B. Jim O'Brien

    C. Matt Bahr (brother of Chris Bahr)

    D. Kevin Butler

    E. Scott Norwood

130. 1984 San Francisco 49ers and 1998 Minnesota Vikings

131. A. Smith

    B. Taylor (Robert Taylor)

    C. Murray

   D. Hambrick (Darren's brother Troy, who also has played for
       the Cowboys, is Mudcat's nephew, too.)

   E. Peete (Calvin Peete)

132. A. New York Giants

   B. Seattle Seahawks

   C. Philadelphia Eagles

   D. Arizona Cardinals

133. E. The Kelly-to-Reed combination ranks third on the all-time
       list with 65 TD connections. Young to Rice is first with 85,
       Marino to Clayton is second with 79, and Unitas to Berry
       comes in at fourth with 63. Aikman connected with Irvin for
       49 touchdowns, which doesn't make the top 10.

134. Charles Martin

135. Stabler—L (1945)

   Zorn—L (1953)

   Moon—R (1956)

   Malone—R (1958)

   Esiason—L (1961)

   Kosar—R (1963)

   Mitchell—L (1968)

   Brunell—L (1970)

   Batch—R (1974)

   Culpepper—R (1977)

136. A. Washington Redskins

   B. Kansas City Chiefs

   C. Detroit Lions

   D. San Diego Chargers

   E. Philadelphia Eagles

   F. Minnesota Vikings

   G. New England Patriots

H. Tampa Bay Buccaneers

I. Cleveland Browns (The Pruitts were not related.)

J. Dallas Cowboys

137. Don McCafferty (Colts, Super Bowl V) and George Seifert (49ers, Super Bowl XXIV). Seifert also won Super Bowl XXIX.

138. B. Ricky Williams had his tear for the University of Texas in 1998. He finished the season with 2,124 yards and 27 touchdowns rushing.

139. A. Oakland Raiders (1968–77)

B. Cleveland Browns

C. New York Giants and New England Patriots. You can also take credit if you guessed the Baltimore Ravens. They won the Super Bowl following the 2000 season, and while technically their predecessor, the Cleveland Browns, lost championship games, the Ravens were considered a new franchise because when the Browns returned to the league in 1999, although an expansion team, the NFL recognized them as a continuation of the old Browns. Therefore, for the purpose of team records, the old and new Browns are considered the same franchise.

D. Los Angeles Rams

E. St. Louis/Arizona/Phoenix Cardinals and New Orleans Saints

140. Tom Flores (1960–61, 1963, 1965–66); Cotton Davidson (1962, 1964); Daryle Lamonica (1967–72); Ken Stabler (1973–79); Jim Plunkett (1980, 1982–83, 1986); Marc Wilson (1981, 1984–85, 1987); Jay Schroeder (1988, 1990–92); Steve Beuerlein (1989); Jeff Hostetler (1993–96); Jeff George (1997); Donald Hollas (1998); Rich Gannon (1999–2002). Lamonica, Stabler, Plunkett, Wilson, Schroeder, Hostetler, and Gannon led the Raiders to

the postseason; Stabler (1976) and Plunket (1980, 1983) quarterbacked them to Super Bowl victories.

141.   A.   Manny Fernandez
       B.   Larry Little
       C.   Mercury Morris
       D.   Howard Twilley

142.   C.   Mark Herrmann played for four teams from 1982 through
            1991, including the Chargers from 1985 through 1987
            before Jim arrived. Mac was teammates with Salisbury on
            the '93 Vikings, Robinson on the '96 Packers, Beach on the
            '92 Eagles, and Bahr on the '89 Chargers.

143.   A.   Roman Gabriel
       B.   Larry Brown
       C.   Bert Jones
       D.   Brian Sipe
       E.   Mark Moseley

144.   A.   Pat Summerall
       B.   Charlie Conerly
       C.   Alan Ameche
       D.   Weeb Ewbank

145.   Denver Broncos

146.   Sam Wyche (Bengals) and Jerry Glanville (Oilers)

147.   Marlin Briscoe and Kordell Stewart

148.   A.   Garcia
       B.   Warner
       C.   Flutie
       D.   Bennett
       E.   Koonce

149.   A.   Ron Moore (traded for Rob Moore)
       B.   Larry Centers

      C. Randal Thrill Hill

      D. Gary Proehl

150. A. New Jersey. Mac was born in Jersey City in 1959. His family moved to California when he was three.

Deep Passes into Double Coverage

151. Billy Joe Tolliver

152. Art Schlichter

153. Kenny Jackson

154. Vince Evans

155. Marion Butts

156. Gary Kubiak

157. Matt Suhey

158. Tom Tupa

159. Louis Lipps

160. Erik Kramer

161. Steve Beuerlein

162. Richard Todd

163. Maury Buford

164. Leonard Davis

165. Duane Thomas

166. David Archer

167. Brad Muster

168. Kevin Greene

169. Earnest Byner

170. Steve Spurrier

171. Craig James

172. Don Majkowski

173. Gifford Nielsen

174. Ray Brown

175. Dick Anderson

176. Bill Belichick (coach) and Mike Lombardo (general manager)

177. A. Houston Oilers

   B. Hank Stram

   C. San Diego Chargers (They started as the Los Angeles Chargers in 1960.)

   D. Jim Nance

178. A. Jay Hilgenberg

   B. Keith Van Horne

   C. Noah Jackson

   D. Kurt Becker

179. A. Oakland/Los Angeles/Oakland Raiders

   B. Green Bay Packers 48, Washington Redskins 47

   C. New York Giants (1987 season following Super Bowl victory in January 1987)

   D. Tampa Bay Buccaneers

   E. Miami Dolphins

180. D. Ricky Watters was a second-round pick out of Notre Dame by the 49ers in 1991; Martin was a third-round pick out of the University of Pittsburgh by the Patriots in 1995. The other players were first-round draft picks.

181. C. Jim Hart. The underrated Jim Hart threw 209 touchdown passes. Next in line were Morton (183), White (155), Sipe (154), and Dickey (141).

182. A. Pat Tilley fell short with 468 catches. The leader in the group was Carmichael (590), followed by Jackson (579), Chandler (559), and Clark (506).

183. Pat Fischer (cornerback) and Larry Wilson (safety)
184. A. George Rogers
     B. Irving Fryar
     C. Steve Emtman (tackle) and Quentin Coryatt (linebacker)
     D. Orlando Pace
185. Luis Zendejas. Tony kicked for the Oilers, L.A. Rams, Falcons, and 49ers from 1985 through 1995, while Max's career lasted about as long as Luis's, from 1986 through 1988.
186. A. Glen Redd
     B. Ty Detmer
     C. Bart Oates (brother Brad)
     D. Travis Hall
187. A. Green Bay Packers
     B. Wayne Fontes
     C. Barry Sanders; he broke the record previously held by Billy Sims.
     D. Chicago Bears
188. A. Marino
     B. Namath
     C. Bledsoe
     D. Bradshaw
     E. Montana
189. Bill Pickel (nose tackle) and Jeff Barnes (linebacker)
190. A. Mick Luckhurst
     B. Eddie Murray
     C. Mike Lansford
     D. Neil O'Donoghue
     E. Donald Igwebuike
     F. Rich Karlis

      G. Nick Lowery

      H. Uwe von Schamann

      I. Rolf Benirschke

      J. Norm Johnson

Lowery played every game for the Chiefs in the '80s except for the three in 1987. If you guessed Eddie Murray, we don't mind if you take half credit because he missed only two nonstrike games in the decade.

191. A. Jim Ringo

      B. 1977—Ken Meyer; 1978—Pete McCulley (1–8) and Fred O'Connor (1–6)

      C. Les Steckel

      D. Rod Rust

192. A. Gino Torretta

      B. Charlie Ward

      C. Rashaan Salaam

      D. Johnny Rodgers

193. E. Pat Riley

194. Charles White (1987) and Greg Bell (1988)

195. E. The NFC team won the Super Bowl for 13 years—every year from the 1984 season (the January 1985 game—Super Bowl XIX) through the 1996 season (the January 1997 game—Super Bowl XXXI). Denver ended the NFC's 13-year run by beating Green Bay, 31–24, in Super Bowl XXXII following the 1997 season.

196. A. Atlanta Falcons

      B. Philadelphia Eagles

      C. Baltimore Colts

      D. Los Angeles Rams

      E. Pittsburgh Steelers

F. Dallas Cowboys

G. Detroit Lions

H. San Diego Chargers

I. Washington Redskins

J. Kansas City Chiefs

197. Bob Griese for the 1973 Miami Dolphins

198. A. Todd Bell and Al Harris

B. Bobby Hebert

C. Sean Gilbert

D. Dan Williams

199. A. Baschnagel

B. Plank

C. Parsons

D. Osborne

E. McClendon

F. Muckensturm

G. Earl

H. Jiggets

200. A. Leslie Frazier

B. Leslie O'Neal

C. Leslie "Les" Miller

About the Authors

Jim McMahon played in the NFL for 15 years. In 1985, he quarterbacked the Chicago Bears to a 15–1 record and Super Bowl victory over the New England Patriots. After that season, he coauthored *McMahon!* with Bob Verdi of the *Chicago Tribune*. He lives in the Chicago suburb of Northbrook with his wife, Nancy, and their four children, Ashley, Sean, Lexie, and Zack.

Dave Brown is the author of *The Baseball Trivia Quiz Book*, which he wrote with relief pitcher Mitch "The Wild Thing" Williams. When he is not collaborating on sports trivia books with colorful former professional athletes, Dave practices law for Levin Legal Group in the Philadelphia suburb of Huntingdon Valley. He lives in the Philadelphia area with his wife, Kimberley, whom he married recently after a quarter-century of bumbling at the dating game. They have one child.